THE GAME OF EUROPE

Swallow Press
Chicago   Athens, Ohio   London

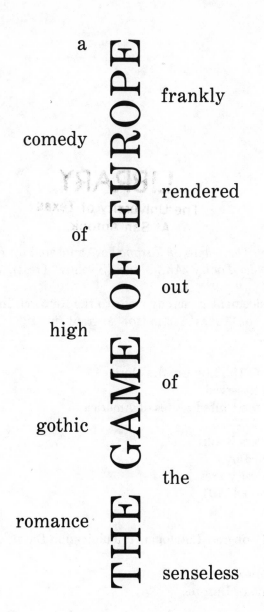

a

frankly

comedy

rendered

of

out

high

of

gothic

the

romance

senseless

THE GAME OF EUROPE

by CHARLES DORIA

Portions of *The Game of Europe* have appeared in: *Floating Bear, Inscape, New Poetry Anthology* (Swallow Press), and *Polemic*.

Acknowledgement is hereby made to the Research Institute of the University of Texas/Austin for a grant in 1971 to complete *rounds 4-7*.

Swallow Press Books
are published by
Ohio University Press
Athens, Ohio 45701

Library of Congress Cataloging in Publication Data

Doria, Charles.
  The game of Europe.

  I. Title.
PS3554.O672G3   811'.54   82-7851
ISBN 0-8040-0409-9   AACR2
ISBN 0-8040-0410-2 (pbk.)

for Diana
and the rest of the family

esto fortis in bello

in ten rounds
with an Introduction

As though a bandage had
been removed from his
eyes, Refo saw—now
that it was too late—
that Plu Toh Ra was not
the superman he had wor-
shipped since his youth.
This was merely a beak-
faced, heartless barbar-
ian who itched for power
with which to aggrandize
himself and his priests.
He tried to comfort him-
self with the thought
that soon his Hellenes
would return to the free-
dom of their Golden Age.
At the same time he re-
called the privation
which had descended when
the factories had stopped.
What if there never had
been a Golden Age?

from *Lords of Atlantis*
      by Wallace West

Introduction

I judged quantity as small because it was small,
because it couldn't have so much as thinkably
been smaller. Spring playing over the senses
never fulfilled the promise made when I was small,
to form an occasion with the higher culture,
an elaborate innocent plan come to nought,
the account lost of that handful of seed trailed
across continents. Hung all my life in a northern
city of declining population I never saw how
I was measured: not by distance from the sun
or my shadow's width, but each year manufactured
on the clock when spring is denied, winter
not resisting the Erie's ceasing tide.

There went my youth, youth in my surrender
on the balcony, in the young man's business,
there all I ever wanted to help forge
the sometime contract her smooth high-held
hands hinted at. Taste so pleased discovers her
anew in the wine or a napkin scented with
its launderings, even in bread, crust
basted with white milk.
                        Both of us fitting,
each confused by all we had which in us
had come alive and taken flesh. Changing
within, walking and wandering I lost all we had,
never having before such wealth from time.
Everywhere I looked I saw ivory and old gold,
and scarce knew where, fearing, to sit, I believed
her the more charged with their use because of
their timeless graining. "After the wars,"
I said, "what? the old days, solid things,
never came back (meaning, kiss me quick)?"

Evening hour yet the daylight hour all night long,
eternal city underneath the flowers, violets,
roses nipping the sense, air suggestive,
vibrant, almost human as nowhere else, active,

becoming, the longer night thickens, of the
texture of things, a design on all I had.

      It is said this way
      in the fields
      climbing back to Perugia
      that gleams above them
      El Dorado in her promise
      of white streets without rain
      and buildings radiant within those
      marked on my trail out back,
      roofs like sunbathers
      on an emerald green
      as the young town
      raises old Atlantis
      painting her eyes fire
      for this dawn's delight
      cocoon on a leaf
      waiting fisted-wing,
      perpetual afternoon

      Gold is lost
      in the apple
      I peel on the hill,
      mold telling
      what it's like to hold
      and shed my scale
      over the cleft trace
      of covenant deer:
      tree rings
      where my time begins
      when I first heard
      Colombo's tale
      to the now I find
      and shiver my axe against

Those first days before the circle closed,
before I learned to repeat so much, flaunted

their affinity with dealers in stamped papers,
rare editions, embossed neckties; recurrently
shameless in the presence of tailors, of
that leisure fully, marking it as if to one
who knew, yet unable to name it aloud,
in the act of surrendering to a swooning world.

You have to be near me
            while I write?
Your hands out
            of my hair!

On the trattoria's steps
a boy hammers caps with a stone
wraiths of smoke hang
like the anger in this room

Doubting, he needs to do it
again, shouts 'ci l'hai
Paolo?' 'si, ancora ci sono
Ma che si fa?'

There women must be either redheaded or blonde,
long-legged or clever and strange, making
the city speak their tongue, and draw such
expressive song I could almost see their forms.

Trees having long since
left their leaves
pater Tiber so high
bridges make ships
sailing against the tide
perishing seaward,
brown and choked
from the uplands:
from my balcony
like a bone from Eden
the German cemetery

inside the Vatican
where Sign. Mattheu waits
'who followed inconsolable
the lovely form of his spouse
a mind of poesy undaunted
among his many friends'

It was in the garden, a spacious cherished
park, tall bird-strewn trees dispensing spring,
whose walls gathering the past, speak of survival,
a strong persistent indifferent order. The day
was soft, we adjourned to air, windows flaming
with late suns, grass bright, wet, the shade in
tatters, bells behind mist tolling from the palace.
I had the sense of names in the air, ghosts
at windows or blazing from yellow chandeliers
buzzing too thick too fast, all windows of sense
down, drinking a tropic light too young to age.
The medallion of her face, every line told
as tone and response, claret glass beaming at him
between her breasts, framed the young man's glance.
Voiceless, she spoke 'this form of sacrifice
will do for the occasion as well as any other'
then in tacit union we turned down the clear archi-
tectural street, leaving small talk with the tisane.

where the lemon trees

pale smoke on the hill,
last act the garden act,
postcard, five-tone plate,
faded lyric pressed
inside a copybook,
changeless oaks crisscrossing
where paths conclude and
hydrangeas, peonies nod
where carnation, gardenia

plain posies all serve
for corsage, boutonniere

memory's daughter
like the poet I have known,
death a young man in the sun
I know smiled on these rounds
remembering that place
miliario uno
where all roads begin,
when her fingers
like spiderline
nerveless, silent
laced with mine:
if I've found
the method of Europe
met long ago in dream,
though perhaps
a game against the rule
of the game,
setting off on that first walk
past carved lions
returning to stone
guarding the path's gate,
black wheels, rain storming
on a far street
after you and me
follow! as if
a novel and this the story,
around the corner,
into the bakeshop, if
you lose them,
who will sing me
Europe, your hope
into eternity?
young woman
young man together,

                    make the shop
                    around the corner

Wherever he looked he saw ivory and gold,
and hardly knew where to sit fearing to touch
the life of their possessor, for it struck him
they were that way the more charged with passion
and pride, becoming an empyrean of things.
This time around the temple's inmost nook caught him
like a wave within a grove revealing nymphs,
curiosities on velvet born to purple and gold,
nothing clear about them save their low glare
of knowledge and time, contempt for the flower
giving way to its worship at the stroke of
their most urgent whim; evenings alive as nowhere
else, questions returning with their answer,
laughter cut short greeting the new man:
'well, they've got hold of you at last,
one could live here years and not dream
such blessing, though not to need it invites
or else puts it off forever, no matter
without you there can be no fulfilling,
no emptying of desire, and that as you
say's it. Now how long you here for?'

1. The Italian Version

I

"I can't. I won't make a martyr of myself."

Unless love dreams it will live forever
it will not last a moment,
if the road will not seem to lead forever,
avoiding the lovely paths we will take
when there is no time, it will fall and end
over the cliffs abruptly, running to the sea
where swimmers have left their clothes
on the beach forever. Come. Here is the gate.
Are you willing to try it? It opens easily,
and the garden (though I know you are sensitive
to the word) sways in its breath
like veils before a fan, and because it is hard
to tear yourself from loveliness, you must.
For here is the path I told you of, there the lion gate:
through it we follow around each tree,
around the oranges and the lemons, quincunx paradise
set forever in rows no matter how we look,
the turning of the stones we have brought to be;
and it will seem they keep us company,
that the orchard was not put here to be burnt
after we have finished and part, but will go on
to house the path, pressing against us
when we lose it, straight and well-ordered
when our feet have lost all sense of the brick,
so that it is our eyes will hold us to it,
shunning the long and fragile sleep which comes
from the dangerous sigh on crags, and oceans
that seem to lead forever south but follow straight
to Hylas' well. For then the version overcomes dream
and turns it spring, coming to our fields
makes it a world which, once we've crossed once,
like Drake we will desire to circle once more.
And it will make no difference if we live
like ants in the earth or can point to our cities,

there is always enough, always enough
once we find ourselves here again, loafing spread
under the shade of a beech, at ease with the grass spears.

II

"you were there all along? wonderful!"

I hear the demon's voice abroad:
'Don't go out tonight. You're bound to take your life.'

Two can be the loneliest number of all.
'Get your things. The end is coming soon.'

The complete freedom to be with her;
but something gone from that now.

Look into the rain forest. 'It is an ice cave.'
Try the anthill. 'It is a prison,' she said.

Dark-eyed moon of the summer night,
take a look at me: I'm stepping out tonight.

There is a part of me that resents my father,
resents what I set before him all unknowing.

And then I vomited, threw something back at them
for what had been going on most of that Fall.

Almost walked out on the stars, six floors
over the street. Got punched in the mouth for it.

Taken by car to the Piazza Navona and dumped
near the shop where Franca did her sewing.

I slept in front of a giant green bottle
the previous tenant had stuffed willow twigs in.

2

Architect, he showed me plans for a house with only one wall
dividing it down the middle. Home that's no womb.

Greek lambskin carpet by the fire place,
a large collection of lamps from Etruscan tombs.

He put on a record of partsongs 'From the Auvergne.'
No, he told her on the phone, I don't know where he is.

'Love without you cannot last.'
Remember Charlie, where you heard it last.

The music out sweeping the streets has dwindled,
now to blood smut on an Eldorado's chrome.

'There is a bad moon on the rise.'
What lasts forever? The sun's an atom too.

III

"I don't give charity"

charity, a little compassion,
that no one should be unhappy, lacking us,
arrests, fixes us
till the arrow strikes in the back again
just as we thought of leaving
and kills us all over again.

where is that great confidence we loved in ourselves,
in that flesh we are born heir to,
that leaving we make our testament,
that makes us believe we were not born for this,
this compact of death's?

after so thrilling an entry,
overturning fort and castle where we hoped to build our home,
where is the iron that is ground off his blade?

the marble worn off the stairs?
for with that iron, that stone,
you will find your father's bones.
all crumb now: knife, marble, skin, bone;
ground down, trod away, they are undone.
they never were.
who knows the revolutions of dust?
dust on king's way, dust on his grave,
they are one: both and neither.
how can it be otherwise?
how can it change?

that we admit the sun's light to ourselves
yet walk love's path towards lying and mean purpose
renders dying meaningless, being born a hoax.
after low birth we pass to honorable life,
reaching past the sentence of meek death
an honorable end which never passes.
but once in the grave
how can we make our worms silk worms?
they were bold and early worms
who ate up Herod before he died:
how much more bold and everlasting those worms who,
after ant and fly are satisfied, remain
eternal feeders of our soul
long after the spoiling of skin and bone by earth-bound worms?

every day shoots a different arrow each hour we remain:
the old man is astonished an arrow from her eye
could pierce him so when he was young,
making him toss and turn all night,
although money lust leads him to a worse place now
then love did then.
a good day looses arrows of meeting under the tree,
a bad day the game of time:
so stay in bed.

4

his whisper will wound you with a stiletta of gold,
strangle you with silk scarves;
smothering in phoenix down, stifling in amber scent,
he wastes you with fortune, ruins you with success,
changing you broken with a twist of his wrist on the wheel,
just when you think you've escaped, the clock strikes;
so abandoning all hope you enter that fork in the road
where he'll gore on one horn or the other:
either to betray someone you say you love
or perish yourself.

nevertheless don't stop turning words to song;
keep peace in your house, peace in your heart.
never listen for music from the spheres,
straining after words that won't fit.

every season has its appropriate dart;
an arrow of the tongue
can wound deeper than love's eye
and make you fare as badly then as you do now.
for a good day brings you to her,
a bad day you waste,
so stay in bed.

IV

"one park bench too many"

San Cosimato
stands in dark truth's time
shuttered stands in the square
huddling against each other
like birds on a beach

identify demand
a place in the memory
or it is winter still

                    among these tombs
                rookery of sea-born bodies

        white days
            Catullus
        have shone
     even for me
            they will not return
                        petaled in gold
        the flame drawn on Roselli's Way
            she stretched over me
                    like a peacock's sword
            to light the road to Maria's church
        now useless! this search for myself
                on the Tiburzi Stairs
                midnight migrant
                    among fair *borghesi*
        ascending to lie down
                last step
            and gaze at her
        hit by dead things the stars

V

"you're early"

If this is difficult perhaps it's because I want the poem
to be philosophical. For me philosophy acts like a thick lens,
joining and separating. The further I raise the glass
from what I know by heart, the more I see a world
of spinning color, good for what I'm not sure. For example
(and this could be the genesis of the opening lines):
one day in the Fall of 1960 I happened to be sitting
in the Roman Forum near Mile Post One, mildly astonished
at the three columns left standing of the temple of Castor
and Pollux, thinking, right, how much they, yes, resembled
those in frontispieces in dozens of used Horace texts

6

I'd seen used in Cleveland for fifty cents or less
and refused to buy. Like magic those half-forgotten lithos
started blossoming in my mind, then faded, replaced
by imperial stone as soon as they became real. And you know,
to this day I still can't remember them for beans.
I saw grass about my feet—saw it wasn't grass
but a split-leaf melilot strangely like our bleeding heart;
I almost expected to find *ai, ai,* Hyacinth's epitaph,
written on the blades. On the distant Palatine it carpeted
the dark rooms of Vesta's Hall where it thronged, seeming
to build Emerald City out of itself it was so thick.
Gliding down the hill it bristled like Moses' beard
among the cobbles of Via Sacra, lending it a faint, pubescent glow.
No mistaking it now: these familiar buildings glimpsed
countless times in paper dreams had lost glamourous power.
This was not me. The wrongness of this earth no geometry
could correct or memory complete—but philosophy might.
For it made everything green a contact point
between what I already knew and what I saw,
turning the Forum into hovering prairie
or a mirror lake where moss and grass tufts float.
If I'd stood up where would I have been?
Where I wanted to be or where everything told me I was?
I held my breath, waiting for the moment to pass.
I noticed the poplars for the first time:
thinking they point to a heaven beyond our own,
they brought me back—to waiting on her love,
finding a place in the city.

VI

La Delusione by Franca Colangeli

"fammi sapere qualche cosa di te"

Molti studi gli costò	It cost you your studies
e il grande oceano varcò,	to cross the great sea,

7

con gioia e allegria viaggiò
e alla meta arrivò.

La gioia per poco durò,
e tutta llanima rallegrò,
sognava agl'occhi aperti,
ma la sua amica lo sa gioco.

Risvegliò triste e inaudito,
come una pianta
dalla folgora
fu travolto

HO! povero passeretto trasognato,
che per tre giorni egli vagò,
come un'acquilone sospeso
al vento di marzo.

In tanta amarezza del suo cuore,
un sussurro le disse, 'vai;'
un'angelo invisibile le avvincinai,
una mano amica vi accolse e vi
              comprese.

Vi aiuto quasi
come una mamma
dalla sua pena
a metterti tutto il bello sotto
              gli occhi.

Quanti ricordi,
belli e brutti,
ormai svaniranno ma la sua
fronte da una ruga resta solcata.

Se la mia volontà riesce
a dimenticare,

with joy and with pleasure
you came to your goal.

Joy lasts but little:
your girl made you her game
while your soul dreamt
open-eyed of her.

In sadness, in silence
you woke,
like a plant
lightning kicked over.

O! poor little sparrow
betrayed by your dreams,
three days you wandered,
toy of March wind.

In such heart's bitterness
a whisper said, 'go!'
I came an angel unseen
and held you tight

To help you from pain
as a mother might,
to set all lovely
under your eyes once again.

How many memories,
both good and bad, must now
go away—but your brow stay
furrowed by one wrinkle more.

If my will succeeds,
you shall forget,

anche il suo cuore
troverebbe la sua pace.

even your heart find
a peace all its own.

Vi aiuteranno a ritrovare
quei che lontani e diranno
il mondo è bello
e val di più di due occhi verdi.

Those who are distant
will help you discover
this world's still fine
and worth more than a pair
of green eyes.

*(dictated to Sig.ra Colangeli by an angel concerning myself
while in Rome—sometime during December 1960)*

VII

cum deliramus, ea numina significamus

Strumming on his lyre the black-haired musician
begins the lovely tale of Ares at his friendliest
and Aphrodite of the loosened hair: how first
in Vulcan's halls secretly they mixed their loves
in the famous house he built of earth and iron
below the sea; and of the many things, disgracing
Vulcan's bed and couch, which came from them.

Instantly the messenger who felt them first
commingle in love and friendship comes to him;
and having heard, heartstricken the god goes
to his forge, building evil in his heart.
On the anvil block he sets an anvil and forges
remarkable chains, not to be loosed, remaining
firm forever. And when angered he finishes
his lures for Ares, he dives into the sea
where his amiable bed lies, and around the bed posts
strews the chains in circles on every side,
hanging some up above from the rafters
which you would never see they're as fine
as spider line, not even if you were one

9

of the immortal gods, for all about the room
he slides his artful traps. When each chain's
been set, he seems, well-formed city-sacker,
to fly toward Lemnos, most hospitable by far
of all his lands, since Ares, god of the Golden Reins,
keeps no blind watch. Once he sees him setting off,
then he starts for the home of the famous god,
desiring at her friendliest Cytherea of the loosened hair.
And having just come from the throne of his father
Cronian Zeus, entering he kisses her on the hand,
speaking in familiar tones, "Once more, friend,
bedwards let us go, and as if asleep find pleasure
in each other, for your man is not at home
but journeys somewhere for his own delight
among the harsh-tongued Sintians."

                              To her,
it seems a pleasing thing just then to be asleep,
and so, stepping into bed, they are asleep.
All about them rain the skillful chains
of the clever god her husband; since Ares
is not the one to lift or move them—those traps
that hold them still, soon they know there is
no escape. The god, metal teaser, comes
advancing upon them, turning back in flight
before reaching the Lemnian land, for Helios
had held his eye upon the pair and spoke the word.
Hephaistos stands by the door, saddened
in his loving heart, fierce anger seizing him:
"Father Zeus and all you other gods eternally happy,
come here and laugh! seeing this absurdity:
how god's daughter Aphrodite dishonors one
who is lame, loving Ares the Destroyer
because he is handsome and whole of foot,
while I have grown up weak and can find none
to blame but parents for giving me birth—
something they ought not to have done.
But see where they lie down in love!

10

curling on my bed while I watch grieving;
soon they will detest sleep and wish to rise,
but I mean to give them hope for a while,
letting them continue in their love and fetters
until their father gives back the dowry
I paid for that girl of his with habits of a bitch;
for she is lovely and worthy love
but her heart is without reins."

Gods gather
in front of the bronze-faced palace:
earth-holder Poseidon, Hermes Helper,
Apollo Master of Arrows, while the femaler
of the goddesses remain at home ashamed.
They come to a stop on his threshold,
these Givers of good things; inextinguishable
their laughter arises once they see
the cunning of black-haired Hephaistos.
One says to his neighbor: "His works are
undeservedly evil: here slow outruns swift.
Sly in wrath Hephaistos the halt beats
Ares the Quick, quickest of gods. And for
what he's done surely a fine is due."

Apollo shouts to Hermes the King,
"Surely, Guide and Giver of good things,
you would sleep on any bed with Aphrodite
of the golden hair, even if you were pinched
by chains and caught in this famous house?"
The Leader of the dead: "You know I would,
Far Darter, especially if you were the one
who watched! o gods! o goddesses! but
let me sleep with Golden Hind!"

Keeping
the joke Poseidon implores Hephaistos Famous
to "set the war god free! And I promise,
whenever you say, he'll atone for all things

11

rightly in the sight of the gods." But the
strong-armed northern god replies, "Don't ask,
Poseidon! Suppose he escapes and won't give me
my money—you know it's me who'll pay in the end."
The thin god with two right arms nods, smiles:
"Course it's not right—doesn't even look right—
you paying for their fun!"

                        Vulcan snaps the chain.
They fly up and apart: she to Paphos,
to the isle of Cypris—Love the laughter-loving,
another sorrow added to her eyes. And there
Graces wash and bathe her, goddess honored
in groves and altars in the flame of holy fire,
smoothing her yellow limbs in oil that is
immortal, ambrosial, in the oil rising
about those who are gods forever;
then they clothe her in clothes,
lovely and wonderful to see...

VIII

"and for that I should get paid"

Stella you should go to Rome,
for your eyes,
too much like a taxi meter,
change with every word I say,
rising to new hitherto unpaid heights.

Go, take nothing with you but your wealth;
so that if they ask you if you're free,
like a princess you'll have brought
a patrimony from afar and can command
the price you choose.
But if they think otherwise,
laugh—tell them
you'd rather be alone.

Last night
it would have been better
if you'd said there was somebody
that you didn't just stuff the money
down a sock with a hole in it.
What's it like,
waking together, discovering surprise!
you haven't lost,
haven't both crept off in the night
each to your corner bloodied, bruised?
When the world outside this room
sprang the trap, it didn't include you.

A disaster, to be hit on the head by a star
(which is as the word says),
to feel the sky sink down
like the canopy in Poe's tale.
We each want something else:
you money, me the black hole,
a little action downstairs.

Yes, you are the forgetting and the telling of tales:
to be imposed on, sat upon, slept on, pissed in.
If you were free, no price would be enough.
I smile, you laugh.
I sit, you lie back.
I'm done, you are too.
Listen born of my cock and wallet womb:

HOW AT AULIS DID THE DELIGHTED DANAAN CHIEFS,
    FIRST OF MEN, STAIN THE ALTAR
WITH IPHIGENIA'S BLOOD? HAIR BOUND IN THONGS
    FELL DOWN HER CHEEKS, FOLDED
WINGS OF EQUAL GRACE. MUTE WITH FEAR SHE FACES
    ETERNITY'S GATE, KNOWING
THE MINISTERS WHO LAMENT HER FOR HER BEAUTY

13

WON'T REVEAL THE KNIFE
WHILE SHE SEEKS EARTH SUBMISSIVELY. THAT
   THE PRIEST WAS KING OF KINGS
SHE CALLS FATHER: HOW WAS IT THIS THAT HELPED?
   WHEN SNATCHED BY AMBITIOUS HANDS
BROUGHT TREMBLING TO THE PLACE OF SACRIFICE,
   NOT IN THE SOLEMN MOEUR OF LOVE
LIFTING HYMEN'S VEIL—BUT NOW IN TIME OF EVIL BED,
   HOST AND VICTIM BY HER FATHER'S HAND
SHE FELL TO RAISE A THOUSAND SHIPS WIND TO WAR

Well, if I keep on jabbering,
you'll ask for another fifty soon
and I'll have to get dressed and go.
If it's hope you want, it's Rome.
But once more into the breach, dear friend,
we don't talk nearly enough—
and this time don't press the grapes for luck,
that's not what they're for.

IX

"when did I ever say no?"

If playful my waves invite you,
if trembling they call you to me,
see how my pool shimmers,
like silk or grass,
repeating stillness,
unchanged by change.

Drinking or washing,
thank the wolf:
her care put me here.

Now Romulus, the truth!
Why keep your mother,
Mars' wolf bride, caged
on the Capitoline?
She only did for you
what she did for me.
And me? I'm no god,
just water and stone.

*(adapted from the inscription
on the fountain in Piazza
Santa Maria in Trastevere)*

X

"You are sweet. You really are."

yes, everything happens to me
and everything happens to you:
no one misses a thing in this world.
For you are always the version
at the height of discovery,
you that is singing *Petit Fleur*
and are the music while you dance,
having it in you until it ends,
no further . . .
who find Spring and the Graces Three
pounding earth one two three,
moving in number from the songs
you give and take away;
the city centering on you,
smaller than a sound,
invites you for a loaf on grass,
asking only that you sing
in sweet and sweeter tones
in the moments assigned,
for she has wearied of voice,

15

for she has wearied of voice,
winds have peeled her walls.
   and you will not go to Ostia
or the *castelli,*
rent a car, leave the city behind,
take a trip and expect a day elsewhere
cast in any other make
than three candles and four walls:
Vecchia Roma, garden of stone,
you were the seed
the first time many times,
for it is time
who makes love pass
and not the reverse;
what has been once
will be again, say the high-held hands;
what the bitch wolf howled
now her fountains murmur
and Mina *cantatrice* cries *'ma tanto, tanto.'*

2. Vienna Chapters

I. Land Swims Into View

If he with all his troop put in

   if boats glide
    under the ranking trees
     and sail's billow in the wind
      catches the steersman's cry

it is still as in the dream

the deep yields up her own

   laden with treasure

   where dragons lie

   curled in sleep

   about them

the white crow a human tongue
  harping at them, edging his way into this scrapbook

  when with all his fleet he puts into port

  from the elements a hint: how many?
   in the garden over the seas
    are the apples golden
    or the men?

   the old world
   hungering for the new

beasts beyond touch go into books
  flames of the snake the rowers sing
   his sergeant beating time

17

a golden age rain cannot age
　　whole it yields up parting like the sea
　　　　countless gates through accidence
　　　　　blinding the mirror lake
　　　　in the valley
　　　　　behind the glade
where the tawn lambskin hides

nailed to the tree, between dragon's teeth
crown for that old serpent time

　　　　　　three, four
　　　　charms of the day

　　　　　　　stop and pace

　　　　　　right, and go north

　　　compass north by northwest
　　　where old Atlantis lies
　　　sunk without a trace
　　　beneath the waves' bier

　　　　voices melodies
　　　　not moving
　　　　stumbling through sleep
　　　　dreaming
　　　　love's kiss wakens
　　　　when snake season falls

what is not of them? not of those who seek?
become of them? coming from them? port and
starboard under heaven is there left one
to give them haven? is that right? is it not

　　　under the sun
　　　　where no harm comes
　　　　　to you in the sun

18

lighting a path
        where no shadows light
            the grave diggers

makers of limbo
        each coming armed
            with a golden spade

four bittersweet young men
        to disinter
            the dead

earth's treasure
        lost in the glare
            behind dawn's brocades

small foot globe straddling colossi looking to her for the answer
the ice queen morning star foam-clad vespera lucifer the wasp
laying her in the empty tomb where moth and dew can't corrupt
they cheat death of victory winning half the time they lose
                        half the game

II. Albumblatt: Kitzbuehl

Birds sing and it snows
then are busy.
many times in the soup
the fruit either dead
or devorant

"she is a baby hotel"

I work the crostic
in the Gaming
Parkstoffe Schlossallee

19

postcards 2.20 AS or 15 cents American
each or five colored, 25 cents for three
Where is Cortina d'Ampezzo

———

The meadows are clear and laundered
I fought in Russland with the Alpiner
sixty miles an hour legs broken
still brave as ever on both slopes
mud on the bottoms despite
imagination they continue
Pfitzner pain killer
dead soup fly
Cortina Lawina
Casino, Kino
Kurhaus, ich bin Gast
50 years before Europe
re-acquires its patina
40 schillings and again 120 schillings

———

Low fire under the corpse
swollen out of dead belly
the formless will approves

———

German slot blur
they toil upon occasion
bear grey improve
the failure to set
properly may cause

———

The low fire flames from the corpse
sits graveyard midnights
the fiddler stamping
crows tattling
their owners stiffening
and the reporters took it up
in 1907 it was Guido Reisch
and then Erich and his wife
Erika, and then it was Reisch's ex.
and then Tony Seiler, then the British
and now the Americans, remarkably sane
if you think about it, Rainier and Grace
do not, and business has never been the same since
Kitzbuehl is near Woergl
home of der gute Gesell's script

———

no, it is not near Woergl

———

For 12 years a blonde
then another blonde
and he turned her out
just below the lift
to pasture
"in that cottage"
more voluptuous and a little stupider
than the first
"and she takes in guests" mountains
and their effects on race

———

in my book
I marked that slope
1951

III. Wienerisch (Apologies H. F. Kulterer)

Kaiser Julius strikes from behind!
Oistrach pays Paganini a bow
Fuchs drinks from Hitler's sieve
    We take the transit!
    Lethe in spring!
    Time divides
    Death whiles
The old man Pounds his tongue in the torrent
spittle tempers his words
that have share of rivers and lakes
I slept in the shadow of Golden Helm
    In Victory no loveliness!
    insuperable loss
    Delight in endless war
    will in the end rejoice
    the world not win out
        in the end
        war in death
          world!
The moon is a wrinkled dug
drinks the sweet air of cafes
in the lair of man proverb
smoke like the ancient crime
    Bale sink! eye heal
From whence this blueness?
Apollo's not this action
crows, lift me as if I were
Corona set upon the lonely sun
lit beyond it poets say
to round our earthen space
    Lights burn!
in the fountains till all hours
until time comes to turn them off
good things from any side
any direction backwards
    Or forward!

             water to wind
             wind to cloud!
Notes scattered
Day Lady cracks
and the crows
depart crowded
Stephansplatz
returning rest
to the Graben
             Cartesius!
             Magus!
             Pyramidus!
             Iamblichus!
Pest soils the mind
that is constant
tuned to stone star wracks
             and down goes Hotel!
             moon sweat and,
             man hollow
             beards root
             King buries
to size the star
weight the fool
to do it open-mouth
             if not the tune
             the action
             rather both!
             and be off
both are gone
hare and hunter
across the Trail
razed in love
to bite the earth
             if not Earth
             then Moon!
             or rather both
Dust rose as if from flower
Moon set burns it off

IV. Epilogue for Dieter Loos

Gloucester who with cold unyielding fold
makes the garden pink and rose resilient
unto granite has grown soft as flesh,
remembering southern seas, siren calls
from divided meadows roofed in grass;
across those stars her poet watched,
atlas of the great dead, in their glare
she catches two stories met in one:
that babysitter who ran to the beach,
leaving the house in flames—no fire,
no baby—but the book's name, important,
supplies the decisive clue: plus this
(as if it counted), plus this in the eye:
"It was a god who rose up over me,
all fiery and fine, on Dogtown Common,
pines crackling like tongues of fire,
the light floating my breasts in air,
no clear path down to sky or sea,
while he drove me back on the tree."
I will not let you rest, enforced
parenthesis, between another's hands,
but who among those standing on the beach,
cursing their luck, knows whose you are?
Our child may die in flames tonight
between her screams, your spasms of delight.
Whose breasts, except this island's
tidal Cut, could have nourished her,
a made-up teen-age nurse out for hire?
This then is not the double case.
Shall I go hungry if trees do not
and deer browse on them? Does light
sleep in thickets with the wolf?
When stars walk: history!

3. Island

indifferent as an eyelid

you fled so bellybone

aeroplane similar to faults

you were a distance

I found myself equal to

[

gas attack

what must
the gammon
have eaten?

]!

the poisonous sting of this caprice

moon-heated betrayal of the tree in blossom

you are speeding down

it is silence
returns
the empty fields

in those provinces which are absolutely nowhere

strangeness crushes our only possible embrace

yielding to the sky a rose idol

insane and decorous as echo death

my mind is clouded because nothing works

         acrobat!

     the elegant conventions
     to which I sacrificed my manhood
     like the balletomanes of desire
     (more ethically than the apples
     around which shadows turn)
     are those robes bear away
     with massive anxiety
     into the bedrooms of dawn
     god makes it there too
     incense that melts
     the ice floes of the sexual system
     in the heavens of my regard

I'm speaking to you of myself the acrophobe

nervous in the caress of my words

how can I blunt time's tooth

or break loose from his jaw?

     Kensington the Church Walk

     I hear the bells

     the great undead poet

     of the cantos knew

clarifying the prompt winter

they lift up my eyes

which lurk in the valleys

of radiant tailings

      what really is work
      with a dedicated blonde
      in the lithe map
      of her ecstacy?

      time slipped
      on milepost one

      a phoenician
      betrays
      the flash
      of her hand
      mooning over
      the children
      orphaned
      in the drift
      of time
      among the figs

I want all my lovers charmed

by these imitations of glass

is not all the world

more beautiful today?

this thoroughness is just a fish

gasping in the vacuum of my heart

a soldier of both sexes

lampooned in gaslight

    somewhere
    and screaming
    tearing away
    with the electricity
    in a violin
    the auctioneer
    of bottles
    hurls a last defy
    at my body
    when junk
    takes hold
    man ecstacy
    cups my balls
    in a scallop shell
    curtaining
    the windows
    of my lips
    retina for a king
    asleep on ermine
    unreeling
    a duel with death
    over the mountains
    that backstop
    neon nightscapes

it's very exciting to write an old friend
while working in a pressure chamber
where some relationship exists between my words
and the life they parenthize

nicer still to hear the phone ringing
provocatively in the back of my head

Island April the whatever '71

dear p c b

(for London wednesday the 28th)

foreign musician
man of profound soul
st paul the alexandrian
rush of all the tsars
head genuinely good
brow inclined
crown tender
in repose
how wonderful
to see you again
how good
you came
to know you would
that you did
a wonder
to have known you
lying all the while
unsuspected
in the grass
like the scent of roses
felt but unnamed
expressing
mystery

the joker lacking in compassion
in sufficient head
without it

29

he speaks?
no friends
no place to
call him home
Sundays in town
a close-barred wit
rolling up the windows
of his low-slung saloon

country man at nine
dressed to it
a swisher
hardly noticed
but ravishing
has hardly anything to do
so refined
france
migod france
you any relation?
absolutely astonishing
intimidating
your lucidity
when it's dark outside

morning the 29th April

mourning blues doing it all
for a bonnye lass
mere slip of a girl
an echo from the gone world
your eyes agates
where I glimpse
ricochet universe
darting out of nowhere

god with the huns
believes in reason
the least expensive way

of getting things done
a studied use of violence
to prevent erasure of his name
does best what comes easiest
fire on the horizon

it's always noon
somewhere in the empire

great bourbon halls
done up in Jacob's coat
on the way to Egypt
(watch out Puritans
don't fall in!)
decent versatile sheep's heads
courting ideas
over a porcelain stove
letters manners
dying of boredom
the siege of Paris
thanks bitch
there was still time
to get that in
siege of Paris
or Florence or Rome
they still talk about it
in school?

good-bye
hooded eyes
glittering in the dark
cat's eyes of the truth
insufficiently restrained
in blindness
how nice you look
with your picture i.d.
dossier in your name
in between manilla sheets

pounds lire
guillotined by money
politics or sex
my maenad priestess

remember me to the pope!
the composer in me denied
heart encased in a box
of native soil
breath a spine
directing the concert
this evening
observed
survived

love

admit it now

you ever see anything like it?

or more beautiful?

the crimson box for sweetness

gliding into it like a torpedo eel in the bathtub

her sheen
clinging
to the shaft
like a pearl's

insinuating my prehistoric generations

into the wrought iron grill work

hoping to scare out of your hole

the lesbian mouse titman

in your half-bombed apartment house

I thrust away deep swathes

in the airy suede of your mount

so pale so soft like Venus by Titian

thin hand

veined linen

ice rose under a sleepy bush

sachet of marsh grass

chocolate cherry

cuneiform satraps
cutting up paper dollies
on the clear deserts of the moon
unroll the mighty bull rush
inflicting commandment
on a non-plussed world

girliecue fantail cerise
rummaging through the dust
of the albatross' contrail

mother window dusk

with that cute tear in your eye

why do you hafta cram

a little yellow pill

down the throat of every passing cloud?

lone

rose

dead

love

        when you first came to Island rolled up in a carpet
        you brought me bouquets of poesie
        and a face full of mad glances

        madonna never foresaw the death
        the insufficiently elated heart
        would die in the theatre
        of her unmade bed
        o great winged cock god
        stab her to stone
        full ass of course
        toking in utter diversion
        of the gal's monikered resource

                I never lived
                more slowly
                than in these
                half days
                which delight
                the pigeons

nesting
on the roof

took months
to get me
back on my feet
memories of home
still deny me
a telephone

spelling
in sign
exactly what
you said
'you're all
caught up
in a venetian
bind!'

     my
but you've
such good
taste

silence
in the rocks!
I'm brooding
economy

I love you for your youth

I love you for the death

you promise me

like a clump of eels! sword swallower

(forgetting you I forget myself)

stinger's bite
then the paralysing rush
aristos' buttie whore
despite your cheap effects
the world didn't get off
get the idea?
smiler in domino
ribbing the beach
the last dream I pun you
in the mother tongue

black justice is slowly

bringing the curtain down

I watch the temple fall

call me Charles Charlie or erk Chuck
I wear an autocratic face
hawk putto nose gnomon of the dial
my ears stay tuned with money
they take their cue from intelligence
my eyes roaming the mouse holes
of this metered room tell time
'this is the twentieth century
a silence that has lasted far too long
emperor meat torn between fire brands
and those who think they survive
renting out the wound it stuck them with
age tested and failed
in the empty jock strap of trench graves
shot while smuggling atoms
through wasp hero runes
holocaust under arm pit!'
I was born antinomy
poetic swan for fire lake

          neck bent a pretzel in law
          thanks to you! aryan super massage

I asked   if loving you ain't right
'where's the Savoy'   then I want to be wrong
he just looked   even if you're just
dagger of a smile   a kiss over the phone
poised to strike   hep   hep   hooray!

     classicism

       unremitting shoot out in the badlands
       10,000 word editorial in *The Times*

       you're silent?
       well so am I

               philology

                    wars and rumours of war
                    watch it passionella!
                    without your strings
                    you'll break
                    just like a puppet
                    love unstrings in the knee

  appeasement english style
  warms the cockles of this chilly flat
  while I bitterly reassure the wife
  that two-faced projector of my will
  I'm not a sub-titled disaster
  breast full of veggies advancing
  like an army in heat on american maid
  so tired I can feel her bones etc etc ache

I'm just another alienated star
inside the furnace of the tree
please blue gypsy dance save me
from the dullness of island
lumbering humble mumble jumbo
her doyens of pap print groan
listening via needle phone
puncturing my sardonic cock

nowadays
when a man loves a woman
things happen
especially
during interrogation

speak!
child of memory
what did it feel like?
I don't remember
invent facts
if you have to
(I never could get them straight
anywho...)

betcha when I'm sixty
I can make beautiful sense
out of all this
but by then
grappling with what new mystery
will I babble!

speaking one for two
hen dia dis
three four hep!

Lucy without you
none of this is true

(even if it was
once upon a time)

obiter dicta
I'm trying hard
to keep it simple

we all want to be
wrinkled adolescents
why grow old?

ooh and it's all right
we're going right back
where we started from
Maiden Agan my love
my eternal love!

a delicate position
I can't put it any better
wanting everything
thinking it nothing

I like machinery that works
and a tight cunt
              yahoo

so what? who cares?

teeeeee yaddada yaddada yaddada yaddada yaddada yaddada

              yoo hoo

      get the idea yet?

      cancel   cancel   cancel

                              peek a boo

            boom

                         boom

([old McElroy -- Ranch!])

    ping   pong

                    voice from the thunder
                    ten long farts
                    You(H) WHo!
                    I see you

        unless the subject of intelligence or death
                        sneaks through the noise

        I surrender to revery
                    raging against the catarrhal madness
                                    of the islanders

                    grey around the edges
        remembering I am a king
                                    (and you too
                    the law is equal to all)

        emptying my life in a mirror
                    I watch pub girls over my half and half

        the window aids my reflection
                    bored as a virgin's haunch

        who are they?
                    can they turn an honest dollar?

        remember Charlie
                    you've never seen anything
                                    more beautiful

                    you must keep them
                                    distinct

                         40

4. Rules of the Game

sure as night

1. in dreams I call love my curse
        driving me in anger
                back to the tree,
   until fate stands on my head, says
                'embrace flame!'

2. one letter makes the dove love
        plowing lillies
        to plant his rose,
        by sword promising
                the garden
        shadow sun shatters,
                pieces
        nailed to the oak.
   I turn against law. heart,
        consider it death.
        love when he's not needed
        returns fire for ice,
                commanding
                my sleep
        to reform his temple
                of trees.

3. since hope leaves nothing to chance,
        sword god stretched over kings,
        give love moments of fire
        when eye searches eyes and
                lips touch,
        fulfill all night those
        prophecies of light
        your sun recalls at dawn:
        'better to lie with an apple
        without deceiving than
        trust the whole tree.

without flowers no fruit;
no seed serving earth
     re-kindles
     your flame.'

4. time advises, time still proves
     nothing has been left out.
     what I desire he pays,
          evening my years
     before I pull short
     on the weights of death.
a leaf in sun's harness I fall
     along paths he blazed;
     shining out red and gold,
     I cast myself in shadow
          on the earth
     face clawing stone:
          idolatry!
     her leaves and roots divine
     from the world before time.

5. star light, star bright,
     venus lucifer,
vain lover of the night,
     beast of two backs,
     cold cock black crow,
     each day you break
          in chains
     on your bed disproves
          the dream:
'open up in the name
     of the law!
spring's the price you pay
     for the freedom
          of my rays.'

6. time can't stop going ring around a rose!
     distracting earth by beasts

42

           inside zodiac tunnel,
        he circles her constantly,
           like a snake bound
      to the poles love shot
      into the heart of her apple.

7. cypress lady, your heart
         pledged oak
where wind, author of all words,
        rustles,
plucking them like harp strings
       out of thin air.
       love's step womb,
       mistress of the wild,
           once bloodied
         salt foam:
in your eyes looms the fate
        severed everyone but you
          from time,
          your father
      not intending you, waves'
          white
          bauble,
jetting rainbows of sperm,
         gold hair,
burning bush branding in water:
        'whoever
          sheds blood
      by woman's blood was shed.'

8. time dying to be born
         you made immortal;
entropy ticking steadily
        in those gears
you call your heart when
sheath smiles home sword
to quicken war in the apple;
        and the tree,

breaking your legs' saddle,
  turns to fall
  in your heart,
leaving in flame the pits
where you sow the garden
  you eat the
  fruit of—
bark gentler than woman
  tickling off
  the snake's slough
when like a salmon
  jamming
  upstream,
he wound up inside you,
sampling the fruit of your womb,
  to sleep
beside his young forever.

9. clouding the mirror belled under your heart,
  witch moon boils and troubles,
  horns lopping heads off waves
  borrow their diamonds from night;
    rubbing the poles
    raw in her cone,
  she makes them smoulder like sticks
    drilled left
    right on a bow,
    hoping this hides
sun's fire which pitted her face.
    lunatic scarring the rose,
mouth a socket without teeth
  she bites through the knot
    petaled in flame
she set as a tongue on my head
telling in blood when the tides froth,
  bubbling through time.

10. I am the spirit
              sheltering
       in this house,
       bound by law
           I see
  what the sun sees:
              each day
         added night
         figures in
  the sum of my years.
              gods die,
         I still say:
  nothing is denied.

10a. trusting his edge love
              inters
       sun's eye;
       striking night
              blind, light-
  honed flint thrusts home
              in the
       bull: hers!
       the sword
  reaming time: rising
              to fall,
         I still say
  nothing is denied.

11. magic when death
       first let me find
              those griefs barren echo,
                     my queen, repeals,
  by impersonation she rules:
  'my mask serves best: you can't
  betray what you don't know.'

12. bowman of the light,
you know what it's like,
                wishing daytime night?

12a. orange skeleton rose,
past promises, lad,
                when the sun arose.

13. princes and kings
                I kiss like wives,
        fiery coals
                who heal my lips:
take me to the mountains,
to the circle made of stone.
        if her twin star
                wins over the bow,
        dreams of passion,
                dreams of blood
                she burned in me,
        must all fade away,
every swallow heading south
                for good.

14. druid priest by partial choice she dances,
        flickering in and out of light
                around the tree,
        marble feet, hands cradling the storm
                feigning sleep
                between her legs.
cracking ice, she pulls the trigger on command,
raining quarrels across the crossbow land;
        mouth pursed up to kiss she hurls
fear white-faced into time looking madly like me.
        gouging out a spear she nestles there,
                melid child,
                and teaches me:
        'pester ghosts until they speak!
        for unsealed by a kiss they'll

give you tongue
to sex yourself in waves of glass,
in flesh fire enters and resolves,
leaving nothing
of you in her.'

15. name for the jeweled hand rising east setting west
every mother's son
takes for his muse,
she records in archeries of light the beauty culled
from wrath, and sowing
the throne
her presence rules
in ivory,
pearl and rose
she stops the young man's mouth with song; against
the lily of the valley
where her court convenes,
he pits his grapes and loses, since by law everything
coming in
a scallop shell is hers.
she even tempts the sun to bridal spread in the grass
under a beech or oak:
whatever dreams she has
for me—must
they lie forever veiled in smoke and mists of flower?

16. if only she drew from life,
I'd be the stars' pupil
and study by their light
her delight
pricking the bride
she arrays in dawn,
when touching her lightly
with a sword
from her inconstant home
she says, 'arise,

                    sweet knight:
            now your rose is mine!'

17. snake tongue cleft talking worm the apple mast
    fickle freckle frotted demon spitting blind the lamp
    beating hide blowing bone prolong the time attempt the sky
    sweet cloven hoof kicking women between the legs honeycomb
    smoke stone twisting cock
    snake tormented snake seduced by pride one half the stars
    red herm garden master locked in Solomon's seal
    pyramid one and only eye backside of a dollar
    tower beacon searching jailor jailed and camp
    cat eye eye of bale basilisk staring freezing stone
    sun son of my antinomies leave depart go
    hide in the sea where law is void and the abyss reigns
            where stars shoot up to heaven's teats
                    drinking milk to glow
    by fear learn fear
    by judgment pain by day day of wrath of woe
    pay your judge the debt by pain you owe
    that wrath in judgment
    name no name names
    calls down on you cast from me
    mask fronting nothing sylphis satyr lar
    hep cat on your mark get set
    three four the door try it go
    twin winning me alone
    get lost this time you lose

18. lullaby and good night,
            lilac lillies of the dark!
uselessly I watched my hour with her pass;
                    with ungainly grace
        I curtsy in her embrace
                    and then awake.
            if I hadn't slept,

                        48

```
            could she have come
                    like the sun
            scattering night?
```

follows day

```
1. sun stamps earth, the ram's skin pulls tight.
        love favoring fire moves me:
                because I have lived
                I will not die.
        silence pity! the snow queen's machine
                nuzzles my hand.
        today we fly to the sun,
        who'll laugh at all we've done.
                now that we've won,
                grass, weed
        whatever springs from woman,
                rains down
                from heaven,
        re-weaves the world and runs
                under the sun,
                ruler of sky
                who sees
how patched in greenness earth rolls out to dance,
        giving back in joy
                the song
        his heart unfolds.
```

```
2. lord and mistress buried behind lips,
        we take ourselves in fee from you:
                no other kiss will do.
        busy all day, soon it is night:
        a voice in the wilderness singing
                'in stillness,
```

             in the long evening
                in the garden
             when nothing is
                remembered,
         I give a kiss you give back to me,
             reckless time
                confounded
                by number.'

3. princess more lily than pearl,
     recalling the moon at your birth,
          those privileges you grant
             in the cloister of your lips
     bind me more to you than the rose
     a magnet draws out of time's iron dust.

4. on a blade of grass startled from ice
     grasshopper rubs his legs and sings,
               'wake up! wake up! why so alone?
               earth again enjoys our home.'

5. at dawn when you open those petals your lips,
     the sun suffers total eclipse:
                    mouth where we expire,
                    smallest final rose
                    of the stars' fire,
                    crowning our desire,
          halo the sun spun blond on gold,
                    paradise unveiled on earth
                    one constant hour –
     my adam unites your eve.

6. unfailing love the prize of those who rob time
                    of the season of their innocence!
          spring given in marriage
                    when stars and all they decide
          divide in two:

                      50

male and female the game played against time's duel
    only you can win!
        smiling sweeter than rose's breath
you'll fall asleep, strengthened by death,
    saturn's planet crown.

7. snow retreats, sun lays bare
    the blankets of my bed,
    showing flowers bees
      and birds trees.
'you're the one I want!'
    spring makes love
answer every prayer: rose
    over the valley
hope believes paradise –
where offered a flame
      I learned
    what the dove means:
'go on take a chance!
      what's
      to lose?'

8. thyme and the lapith remind the apple of my eye,
    'so what if he wears your heart
      on his sleeve,
      your name on the page
      woven into song?
when like ice and snow we're marred
      by time?
    lips bare teeth,
      breasts hang,
    cunt goes dry.
then he'll do what he does with us,
    throw you headlong
    down earth's womb,
      an omen
    weaned from the fall.'

she listens, she weeps. silence birds!
while I track like
a beast
the changes her heart
takes.

9. buried since birth in the heart her cry
rouses that death rattling my
bones I'm always the first to woo:
'whoever wins the long argument with you,
death, the last word?
I may be candler to the stars,
once beggar sex crosses my palm with yours,
I cold cock from the pubes
hard as glass,
shivering flowers off flesh I leave
numbed and lewd.
why make time's wound law
when love will make you die by shutting
that gate, kicking away
the scaffold of the world?
you starred and starred spreadeagle
in the sky
so rose knight can wink,
paying in continent what riddles you at sea:
hep four two three!
even sphinx, queen's pander, can't fix that.

10. death, your bounty is revealed
in the lily
fading to water
after heaven's fever
whom you'll marry me to
in the grave,
lured there
by her colorless perfume.
for you alone answer me!
placating the rest

                    abiding
            by your dust.'

11. love hidden in a cleft of air,
                spare me this evening,
                I offer you odds
                    against dying.
                like a bride in red
                she camouflaged
                    in cupid,
    changing into a cloud too bright
                    for me to follow,
        she withered my arm in denial,
                    so now
                I can't bend the bow.
    girl forgive sometimes or else
                    confound
                the names we have
                    for things.

12. and above all don't turn your back on him!
            or springing up from behind
                like a stag in rut,
            he'll break your heart:
                    his arrows never miss
                    those you kiss.

13. whatever we intend,
            love's son mirrors;
        his fire flowers in the night
                need our plucking,
                    charmed by the song
        you gave yourself to me,
                blond thrush
                        lipping the void
                        sky tore in time.
        death winding spring
                around earth:

wake coiled eyes
where cupids
can sow their lusts,
find shadows
for the crow,
blinding them
down a slit in the hill he pretends
to bomb so
he can build
his nest there.
earth husbanding me yoohoo
your eye
explodes!
I see you –
city twin
found in time
spelling out my name.

14. in solemn spring
what her eyes dictate
I take for my truth
beyond memory or desire;
from the newness of things
a sleep without death
won't let daffodils and crocus forget
'the flower crushed by lies
will never be untrue:
love any other way,
you'll break on the wheel.'

15. when moon lifts up her lamp of glass
to beg her brother's light,
wind shredding every cloud
sways my heart like a tree
this way and that,
forces open the lockets of my eyes
to fields and rivers,
antidote for sleep,

where dew rises rivaling the stars,
        easing a mind
    almost trapped by time.
suddenly boiling up from below like a madness
      I can't contain,
flame breaks through the veil,
       disguised as love
        to murder thought.
nightingale, my minstrel high on a tree,
      sings how 'the flower
      I fell in with time,
relit rainbows after the flood,
      obeying first water,
        then fire.'

16. changeless for an hour of rage
I am become death who never dies:
love, turn back the clock's hand!
      renew my years in the garden,
        I'm not sure spring
        can deliver the mind.
    the guinea sun dreams his sword
impales again without touching skin,
      committing the season I learned
        to fear love:
      eye in the flower
      evenings and mornings,
        spring,
        the first day,
     light from darkness,
dear heart, you always come back.

5. The Fields of Luxembourg

the

green

corners

the

earth

colors

covers

the

grey small

sea

brown   purple

                        green

     earth

                        small

                                          grey

                        sea

green   brown

                        purple

     earth

                        grey

                                          small

                        sea

purple   green

                        brown

     earth

                        sea

                                        grey

                        small

                        small

                                      sea

                        grey

brown purple green

        earth colors

    sea covers

        small grey corners

            of earth

earth of

        corners grey small

    covers sea

        colors earth

            green purple brown

of earth

        small grey corners

    sea covers

        earth colors

            brown purple green

green colors

        cover grey

    purple sea

        brown earth

            small corners

purple corners

        color grey

    brown sea

        green earth

            small covers

brown covers

        corner grey

    purple sea

        green earth

            small colors

brown purple green

                earth colors

    sea covers

                small grey corners

                        earth

green brown purple

                earth covers

    sea corners

                grey small colors

                        earth

purple green brown

                earth corners

    sea colors

                small grey covers

                        earth

purple brown green

                covers sea

    colors earth

                corners grey small

                        sea

green purple brown

                corners sea

    covers earth

                colors small grey

                        sea

brown green purple

                colors sea

    corners earth

                covers grey small

                        sea

brown

                                        colors

                sea

                                                corners

                                                        earth

green

                                        covers

                sea

                                                corners

                                                        earth

purple

                                        corners

                sea

                                                colors

                                                        earth

purple

                                        colors

                earth

                                                corners

                                                        sea

green

                                        corners

                earth

                                                covers

                                                        sea

brown

                                        corners

                earth

                                                colors

                                                        sea

the
earth
colors
the
small
grey
corners
of
the
sea
brown
purple
green
the
earth
covers
the
small
grey
colors
of
the
sea
brown
purple
green

the
earth
colors
the
small
grey
corners
of
the
sea
brown
purple
green
the
earth
covers
the
small
grey
colors
of
the
sea
purple
green
brown

the
earth
colors
the
small
grey
corners
of
the
sea
brown
purple
green
the
earth
covers
the
small
grey
colors
of
the
sea
green
brown
purple

brown

        the

   sea

           grey

             earth

               colors

brown

        the

   small

           grey

   sea

               corners

purple

   sea

   small

             earth

               covers

purple

           grey

   small

   sea

               covers

               corners

green

        the

             earth

           grey

   sea

               colors

green

        the

brown   purple   green

covers   corners   colors

small   grey   sea

green   earth

6. Actor Scan

- -
- -
- -
- -
- - - this english - - - - - - - - - - - - - -
- - - - is for Tim Reynolds - - - - -
- - - who always - - - - - - - - - - - - -
- - - - - - - -serves first - - - - - - - - -
- - - - into the fishnet - - - - - - - -
- - - - - - - - - of light - - - - - - - - - -
without tangling - - - - - - - - - - - -
- - - - - - - - the cords - - - - - - - - -
- -
- -
- -
like a stork - - - - - - - - - - - - - - - -
     I am many jointed
my name is arrangement
- -
- -
watch out - - - - - - - - - - - - the
        telly can
carry you off
       in its belly
can pouch - - - - - - - - - - - - - - - -
- -
empty doors
       & rooms - - - - - - - - - -
can open
- -
where can I stop?
- - - - - does first matter
    if there is a second
     a hundred thousand
held fast in the deep
      of my heart
which with fact - - - - - - - - - - -
- - - - - - - out - - - - first - - - - - - -

through the fiery world
       I can hear
the sick returning
       of the wheel
- -
- -
if you don't know it
       you got it
take another piece
       & be off
with you - - - - - - - - - - - - - - - - -
- -
when there
       will be no lost
who will be
       my my
- - - - - - - - - - - - - - - - - ? - - - - - - -
behind glass light hides
       I am
the silhouette of
       my eye
there the story goes
    if it makes you
    that's how
       the heart breaks
in the cabinet of the
       old telly
caught in a second
       that can't make
the turn - - - - - - - - - - - - - - - - -
       like a worn spyglass
I fold in - - - - - - - - - - - - - - - - -
- -
- -
I went to the store
    to get some more
came back and was gone
- - - dogs - - - - - - - whine

on the dyne of
    fine spiderline
where will I turn
- - - - - - - - - - stop - - - - - - ? - - - -
Tim says
  that it does not ever
does not mean
    it will not ever
how does it come
    you the poet
could not fight
    carried over
  from da da
  how many
have you slain

- -
- - - - in the thickets
of my mind   ?
    you found
blood reigning
    the strong grain
heaving
    weaving the
    matrices of
interstellar spaces
- - - - - - - - - like a fool
I flooded the room
  with baseness
    of tongue
  you had
to shut my trap   I
  walked right
    into it
  double dip down
    the middle
I can snuggle you too
  had not expected it
to go on like this

                    three times
a flop
        I took to flight
in hilarious sense
- -
- -
Frank
        In sense
                & Mirth
gifts
        magicians
                        bring
I found under
        the tray
of my soup - - - - - - - - - - - - - - - -
- -
resume the
            argument
think in paras
        that's not my
                style
I heard
        correctly
I am obstinate I won't
                    perpetuate
        a bastard line
worn out
        on old LIMEY'S
                rock
you need me
            to know me - - - - - - - - - -
- - - - - - - - - - - - - - - - - -no! it's
                not too bad
I cannot find
            it   it just
can't be - - - - - - - - - - - - - - - - -
- - - - - - - but here
        we find ourselves

in *mezza età*
       waiting for
the frolics to begin
     we write
ourselves in
       but the devil
he say no
       it's just
not so - - - - - - - - - - - - - - - - - - -
- -
- -
Jim Wiseman
     is part Cherokee
and so's his wife
      Stanza &
        refrain
- -
in my fathers
     there are as many
          like me
ooh but it's good
     just to sit
and break your ball
      balls for food
- -
- -
- - - - and stoop to it
      Charley Old Boy
there may not be
    always
another time
     to pick the flowers
       standing there
     in January
but will you
    find them
- - - - - in time
- -

baby -
                          don't stop
I see where
          you're
          going
I'm not interested
                in a trip
          without the tariff
I find your interest
                more baffling
than prolonged
                imagine
what I could say - - - - - - - - - - - -
- - - - - - - - - - - - - - - - - - -if this
- - - - - - - - - - - - - - - won't do
- -
tomorrow
     the sun shines
moon glows
          birds do
the expected
          I turn over
     still asleep
getting ready
          to light up
the day
          my black heart
               breaks
- -
- -
there are no crooks
          except
     what's left
          of you
my version of you
          which I won't
               let go
          until it's true

72

                    & you see fit
- - - turn me in turn me
                              out
I sit back head
        in my hands
there is no rest
          in these many - - - - - - - - -
        one of these many - - - - - - -
        out of these many - - - - - - - -
                someday - - - - - - - - - -
it all
        catches up - - - - - - - - - - - - - -
what I keep back - - - - - - - - - - -
        until I get back - - - - - - - - -
jump & catch
          chances - - - - - - - - - - - - - -
        story ahead
of time - - - - - - - - - - - - - - - - - -
                can't harm
                you here
                (parenthesis)
                between
                my hands
- -
- -

twice a day
                              at least
my brain turns
                dust
                trundles
out my ears
                death's wheel
rutting my head
- -
o moll star of saturn
                        ring me
            like telephones
lap me

                    73

       in egg water
dropped
     from the celestial
hangar - - - - - - - - - - - - - - - - -
- - lights off ! - - - - air - - - - - - - -
- - - war - - - - den - - - burn me
- - - - - - - in effigy - - - - - - - - - - -
someone has given me
               gift!
Mozart said
             when the muse
left
             unstringing him
over my head
           the semaphore
     Seraph sans Serif
            comes down
is torn
      the train
didn't jump
      the tracks
- -
- - - natural order
    is not subject
no matter what
     we do to it
wisdom persists
     outwitting
       time
on the night side
    of the moon
they're not waiting
    for my come-on
they know - - - - - - - - - - - - - - -
- -
think it now
        - - - - - - - - - - - - -
          they've got it

behind each woman window
   stands
      the telluncular
wisdom of what each
          might be - - - - - - -
- - - - duck - - - - - - - - - - - - - - - -
- - - - - - - - - - - the phone - - - - -
what is all right
      is enough
down the paler black
     of my head
    not so cold
    as I thought
there perishes
    the unexploded
    shell
    of my heart
I will shoot if - - - - - - - - - - - - - -
      at - - - - - - - - - - - - - - -
shoot! - - - - - - - - - - - - - - - - - - -
           twice
Sickle Stork
    refused
      my child
like a widow's house
       he opens
        nightly
closing with a slap
     at death
   his butt
- -
- -
round and round
   you can't go wrong
in my song
    there are tales
for a thousand ages
   yet to come

be there
                gather them in - - - - - - - - -
death the bougar with
                those dumb black
                                boots on
I run your tricks
                of tongue
ease &
                easy undeterred
out in this
                how in this
why in it
                how they make me
fit
        ? ? ?
                        down
the expected road
                there is nothing
left unturned
                not   even   a   stone
                                on stone
the worms
                have all gone
fishing
                for the stork
try this fork
                open the can
spaghetti belly
                you can't take it?
don't try
                and make it
work
        jerk
                        cock your
                holster
stand
        will stand me
the mad monster grope

                    go
cave
            inside me
ditta dot dit
            banging the keys
        any which
            way
hear it sing
            rings around Rosie
Gert with Saturn
                    Crone Sky
makes mine pie
                kick your heels
and fly
                    lil ole blow worms
star fish inch fins
                weasels & mice
honey bunnits &
        brindle fowl
            running for the
                    money
- - - - - - - -greenleaf
whiteman
                and the settler
gambler
            hep d p soft
        shoe piano dancer
man woman
                    made to flesh
against the laying
                of the sun
            all the world's
no home for you
                o yes my friends
        in all the world's
one place for you - - - - - - - - - - -
- - - - - - - right or wrong
                ding dong

77

I hate the woman
            who'd make
your life to blame
            cut - - - - - - - - - - - - - -
            woman - - - - - - - - - - - - -
invite me along
            one two
            who's got
        ?   into you - - - - - - -
- - - intact - - - - - - - - - ! - - - - - - -
racked in Austin
            Stone Age
        upon me
        I wander the
            Valley of Cool
                    mourning
jokes and
        marmalade
up my date
                    yep
        you're probed
    the sky
is known
                        round & round
my soul

like a mouth   I go

                        to your den
I'm going to take you
        scribbling
        leaves
until it all
        comes back - - - - - - - - - -
- - - - - - - - - - - - Crow Wheelie's
back from
        Capistrano
            parks ruts
        in my skull

come spears
   fire tongues
     up the anus
like the fountains
   of Versailles
if ya pleeze - - - - - - - - - - - - - - - -
            so stay ahead
         paint a yankee red
he'll break out
            gold and roses
while you talk
   death slides
his crotch in my head
        hides me
   for what he can get
- -
tsunami
   that's Tim's
about this one
     so long
   I didn't
     dedicate
(see him)
        till now
   fast head refreshed
by transient grapes
   I press against
     my lips
tongue   a black snake
    hard
      skinny
I grind
   into you
  o
lovely speech
   flakes out
the stinger
     (will - - - - - can)

79

                    fan down
                  your pistol
            so we can
                  shoot it out
            before I come - - - - - - - - - - - - -
            - - - - - - - - - - - - - - - -down - - -
            - - - -I can make- - - - - - - - - - - -ten
            suits - - - - -one dress - - - - - - - - - - -
                        eyes gone into
                              holes!
            catch the light
                  before
                        it dies
                              in stone
            leftovers save
                        for your peeping
                  whining and dyning
                        the same old grr
                                    grass
            no gyrene
                        on one hand
                        or the other
            will bring you
                        home
                        longer
            than you care
                  to stay - - - - - - - - - - - - -
            then you went out
                        to string
            - - - - - - - - - - -
                        strange
            how it takes you
                        time
                  ing & raw
            planned ulcers
                  send this off
            to the cramp in
                        my brain

                  80

              your kinks
          don't wow me now
   Snap the Dragon
                 puffs
   Chain Train
            pulling me
               down the
            sparkling rime
   riddled world
            & songs
                 with bullets
   twist my muscles
            to cat gut strings
   xylophones
   - - - - - for bones
                 - - - - - - - - - - - - - -
   help me
                 helmet of my heart
            to lie to you
   as we go
                 through
                      Barbel Meadow
   where I'll crouch
            peeking up your
            armadillo thighs
                 - - - - - - - - - - - - - -
   - - - - - - - - - - they are
            a devilish
                 nation
   without numbers
            without games
   arid in
            blameless
                 sleeves
   who learn
            taking by being
                 going off
            like clockwork

if they're to make
        funnels
            choral or
        a Zen
        chime
                - - - - - - - - - - - - - -

seas rise
    in serpentine
        might
upon the endless
            homeless
house-starved captives
        Grand Cod
        gallops to the
            grave
before those angels
        forethought
            crazes
scale their souls
            laughing - - - - - - - - - - - -
hail the
        vision
        mocked up
            by Belly Can's
            four-in-hand
Holy City
        rarely there
            shaking fretting
the chill in our lines
        so stiff
you are but breath
                points
        from death
        no fast way
        round
Mile Stone One
    -
    -

- - - turn around   - - - - - - - - - -
- - - - - I want to   - - - - - - - - - -
                - - - - - - - catch the light
before it's down   - - - - - - - - - -
- -
BIG BUTTER
        Ramsey - - - - - - - - - - - - - -
                  assist
              this preparation
never a fly
    on you
        sitting still
listen slowly
        master of
    the undetermined   here
the pieces whir!
- - sky - - write - - them - - -
    in the fathomless
        blues of my heart
loose-loop pearls
- - - - - - - - - - - -
O MELLOW man
              Butter - - - - - - Pole
              Ramsey
            Peg o my heart
show us what
    we are
behind the mirror
    of our womb
                  men
high & low
    I searched for this
          when it
          came why'd
    I say no?
each night
      your agents
      Cantank Skunk

                Tortoise Belybon
                        visit
Exquisites
        the pair of them
                battening
                the heart
undeterred   death comes
                quick
                gowns
                    my two eyes
in Earth's paisley
                    I will come up
            rose
                        or sage
pretending
            it's not time &
it all goes - - - - - - - - - - - - - - - - -
            wrong - - - - - - - - - - - - - - -
I am ground to
                Earth
            floored by her
                    acreagé
minions of fair
                    marionettes
                debase
stuff them with dirt!
                    decree
                has come
            to the misused
                    briar patch
where I tear
            my flesh awake
                Edison's organ
            bits of glass
share the tune's
                calm light
            even the mercy
of the least beast

shatters
at twelve
predictably
like a worm
on the line
Dom Clock
strikes
hands up
everybody!
hooking into
heart's
everybody!
hooking into
heart's
every nook

- -
- - - - O - - - -
blond - - - - blond
BLOND
!
shuttered beneath
grass
I'm dreading those rays
Stork
bets mates howling
'double or nothing!
(mostly it's nothing)
when I come
through your rose
sun's DIAFRAM fill in
our_____make
blank
room at the inn
no it just
can't be! dying
before finding
womb's light

- - - - - - - - - -

```
      - - - 2 - - - - 3 - - - 4 - - -
- - - - - - - - - - - - - hep - - 1 - - -
I went to put my
      arm
      around the branch
            of MOLTING MAN
dear Gangster
      of my deprivities
            cursed
            when he first
                  found out
now I lie
            forever mired
      in dreams
worm
      at my heart
                  Stork le Croupier
                  on egg cobbles
                  flaying a stained
                  white mule
7
      ways            - - - - - - - - - - - - -
- - - - - - - - - - - - - - - - - - - - - - - - -
- - - - -                      dusty pass
- - - sun - - - - - - day - - - - - - - - - -
- - - rosary glands
      - - - - - - - - -          totals
I will never
      make it
amount to more
            than what
      you have already
given
      even I
            figured it out
just as you foresaw
                  it would
now Puddle Earth
```

show me the door
until again!
Glair Eerie Loo
rolling crap
on the shores
where
you've been
stranded
and you once
mine
Clove City
splitting your
sides east west
river bends
I'm a-leaving
this time
not finding
these words
in me before - - - - - - - - - - - - - - -
- - - - - - - - write them in
you're looking
good
such things
as legions
may you read
but gulls
can sweep
between the eyes
brain
throngs the
whirl dyne
spinning holes
from sperm line
Venus
to my Mars
mannering it out
alone
before the music

                    turns
who will call me
        if you don't
see me before
            I go
        tonight
run it out
        in spiderware
                rain of
                pearls
        I'm up
            to kill
        once I deliver
                right
            from wrong
hell
        has made me
                whole
walking a crooked
                    mile
under the stars'
            blue glaze
when joints crack
        letter it out
                flash
        in my face
            you feel so good
                against the rocks - - - - -
                                - - - - -
                                - - - - -
                                    death
- - - also the flowers'
- - - - - - problem
                        - - - - -
    -
    -

I have given heart
      to this lovely
            torso
- -
- -
- -

7. <u>Wasp</u>

shaking their white asses
   I go pale
  tawn bodies
snapping under the black lash
    wasp
   reclothing his stinger
in the gold singer
   on bad rock

  only the chased
   & unchased
 can know the difference
   know for sure
 which one
   they are

 carved and uncarved
   caring & uncaring
 this message
   on their brow

 crying love's
   ancient lament

 'yer candle's
   almost gone!
   time for my machine
   yes wind twist grease it
 to please it kiss it squeeze it
your sweet pet's design no not the reason
   piston clouds perpetually frown
lightning that old timey fraud like a tin reward
   jerking her chord
   pay squeak board
etched by scoria of countless bad theories a go go

why not blow pogo
at the tip of tierra del fuego?

the fun of it's not the sum of it
I will make you a ton of it
fall up spring back
on the playful hump of the sun of a judge up
next to the map of it snap it up
flaps down flick out
between nubs of it flub a dub rubbing her nap
knuckle in bud against butt of it
flood a dub dub bub
her blood on the bulbs of the rocks
skinning its gears
lever a starboard the rubbering up stuttering up rudder
juggling her tits
tired of it? mine
that butte of a cunt lip so nice
mice dice for it
till sand dollar eyes meet you in water
denying your shearing
will cost you the fleece'

no matter what reason

love does not stay

but for the season

though I yearn for it

this will not change

god does not come

on a plastic spoon

pit her back
yell her black
hour glass widder at tat
fat cat pussy 'wilder my back yard
reams all night Dad A
not too hard to figure who'll gig her
mack who's that running in the roses
blowing up hoses nose in the dove
shoves his pistol against changeless shoals
those coral thighs
ringing the goal

beats me why I tie my bones in widow's weed
still green in the fall
lies when they're knotted
cries if they rot
like the beating of the sun
you poured across my knees
I'll be needling you
once the gum shoe cracks
grrrled cuticurls on the ash wrong end up
of course if montague capulet racks me
I'll scream
my silence's your dream
without it try telling
pictures from cream
how time fools luck!
the bad hand won
rands or bucks
does it matter?
who stole our fun?
if you can make what I mean
where in my intention the green tip comes
I'll stand and deliver

impractical heaven

come down from the dew

obedience against the flaw

cost man child dearly

for there's your last home
european
by air you're pinned
sea water pond
hand lard uppers' friend
so tired you bawl for a banker's brass grin
defrocked
totally in hock
even milord's cock
forgetting your lib lady's past
you just muddled along
slipped by
squandering
mean borrowing your brothers in sin
o my cavalier iron clapped on horse
you did it all for love
bundled sticks on your rod
reading 'strength through joy'

preaching to the cold winging the continent
the unchased nymphs of morning age
when love's scythe breaks in agony on the rocks
flint the father of their child
ice blue blond on a bear rug
soft backed dimple cheeked thick
hands and ankles
eyes hung bean pole on a stick
tight on an island
you'll keep busy legal clean

94

                    prying out secrets
          european man mountain dog
               peckerwood wick dyed
                       in baptist wells

     GOLDEN AGE

     deliberate this time!

that fool in his tent
          unmoved by your temptings
     saw in pastures of sky
daddy lions police the high men lining
               his wife's gadfly
     lifting her skirt he christens her
          lily-of-the-field
                    stooped-back-valley
     past the lips of her lawn
               jack takes queen
     to learn why iceland island
                    is a land
          where walls can mountain
               typhoons fountain
                    1   2   3   beginning to end
          whirled in the same womb
               mount her rut
               redress for the sun
     covenant deer must honor on stone
                    discovering home in a flower
                    wind pulled bare

     iron wheeled faker

     cover her well

what a team you'll make

twisting the last rhyme

accorded ice

from the bone white fingers

of ladies garment girls

out on a late night

cutting come short

before their wedding bells

too late
  why couldn't you wait?
   jail bait born to purple night
    get in tune to the straight piano
     for where you sit wisdom persists
   until you fire
       so quick to greet dawn
      sinking once more atlantis ark
         shield of my house against yours
    carving an empire out of the garden
      whose sun never sets
     claw law in the belly of your sails

virgin queen

lord of the sea

china poppy

black madonna

cornsilk made

indian pearl

knitting in

sex's refinery

man rises from the dead

taking woman for his bread

this is the first hour

this is the last

blue bonnets white hats

thievings by birds and men

the actors of this tale

wasps shoring up sand

hard anticipation of my song

'fly away

little ones

darlings of the hive

just death marking time

is left is right'

8. Palace Rooms

unlike you
young man
I'd never have left

the message
against silence read
'gods will walk again
when men are dead'

that's where you
went wrong son

body prints fashion
later deny this world

tree limbs lifting
song like wind
my lips' offering

young and old
bark clothed
muscles lining skin

times I leave myself
unborn under the tree

leaf cabbage
thorn rose
a bolt of silk

girls decline the mother
they can never have
childless
they hate the land
they never lived

does light sleep
in their mirror
a stag in thickets
with wolves?

the palace capping chaos
drains the flood

running earth

it thinks!

green or white?
angel can't tell

spring
the law of flame

prophets!
no more presidents
or kings!

by body
track the gods

hand
in heart's surge
confound fact

when I cry
who will hear me?
every angel is terrible

racing the wheel
angel allots me

going
like an oracle
either way

up down
all direction
divined from birds

meaningless signs
along the road

left out of children
outside playing
with a dove

pointing me out
too young too old

(it) matters
where words go in

between them
I plant you
seeming rose

your most active
'Joshua fought
at Jericho'

these lines membranes
filming tides

Jerusalem lost
who's hep?

high in the wings
fate depends
through the veil
night descends

passive love's
four letter word

if this is difficult
it's the way
the world goes

habitually sending
angels through
hell's body wick

scoring the waves
words heal

they figure
the sky-borne ladder
earth turns on

up where
apples fall
the milk road
winds home

lion or lamb
which Troy's down?

coins sectioning
the light stream

swimming by March
wind clones eye me
boy swans ride
across water

creatures
half bone half toy
plotting rooms

without womb
impossible!

trading temple
for bank

entropic tomb
daughter of time
you're breaking me down

thorn bud rose
rising to fall
not standing still

king's law confirms
yes!
departure is by design

to snap the chain
heart
stand and deliver

a cultured palace
around the corner
offends the eye

once upon a time
sons left the pale

heaven
earth's veil

outlaw angels
stroking flame
your claw in my soul

I grow hot I grow cold
the closer it is to blue
the nearer my god to you!

unless tomorrow
comes today
the spell's not complete

not yet born
mounting the rose
with an arrow
he turns it gold

wide face dual waist
bows mourning east
he reasserts
the empire of dawn

less than east or west
spitting down birth's spring
yet when mimosas blow
lips obediently bow! wow

u   p   c   b
birds like angels go
hep   hep   hep

9. Atlantis News

Austin April 1973 ..... hand in hand .... through the moonlight ... roses and violets ... stay with me tonight ... school board president Will Davis said Friday the public has responded dramatically to an announcement last week that suggestions for the naming of three new schools would be welcome ... the names submitted include L. C. Anderson, Lyndon Baines Johnson, Dwight David Eisenhower, John F. Kennedy, James Bowie, Albert Stanley Burleson, Martin Luther King, Sam Rayburn, Homer Garrison, Walter Kock, Freddie Steinmark, Sam Houston and Oral Roberts ... Davis said, "The board is not running a popularity contest ... we are not dominated by the public viewpoint. It is a matter of the board's prerogative and decision" ... Italian president Giovanni Leone said in an interview ... "women are the most beautiful things...... in ... the world ... the strongest evidence that God exists".... a 7-year-old girl keeps asking everyone in sight, "What's going to happen when I die?" You can't just tell her to go out and play because this little girl is hospitalized, dying of leukemia... physicians all too frequently avoid answering entirely by saying something like, "I hear my page; I'm too busy"

.... nurses .... often adopt a strong parental attitude, scolding, "Don't talk like that; take your medicine and you'll get well." This is not only a lie—and the patient knows it—but it makes death seem like a punishment for being a bad child ... a seemingly hostile attitude on the part of the healthy person stems from one's own unconscious fear of dying... answering a question with a question, "what do yo think will happen?" ... the little girl replied, "Why, I'd fall asleep and wake up with Jesus and my little sister (who had died earlier of the same disease)" ... a picture drawn by a dying boy showed a huge tank bearing down on him. He drew himself holding a stop sign ... he drew a peace bird, heading skyward, its wings brushed by light ... "where did Kenny go? ... where where was he, Mommy, when he got dead? ... I really liked Kenny and I'll miss him a lot. He only did die, like we all do someday. So long, mommy, I'm going out to play" ... "you're going to take me in an ambulance to the place where Beth Ann ... is" ... be sure to "put on the light in the ambulance and run the siren very loud so that Beth Ann knows I'm coming" ... there was a calm little boy whose only idiosyncracy was ...

keeping an apple outside his window ... "maybe Mommy (who loved apples) will come back and not be mad at me anymore" ... "be suspicious of the 'super good' child ... fifty years later he may ... be ... determined to suffer for his childhood crime by hurting himself." The "crime" ... of having 'killed' the parent by wishing him or her dead, sometimes a child's only way of striking back ... to the very devout father of two leukemia victims ... a priest said after the death of the first, "God needed little girls in heaven and He chose your daughter." When the second daughter contracted the disease, the father took her to the hospital and abandoned her, saying, "God, would you like to have another little girl in Heaven? You might as well take her now." He never once visited her ... some of the neighbors ... were shocked ... when Mrs. Jones ... let her 6-year-old daughter and a playmate view the body ... of a terminally ill bachelor ... invited ... to live in their home ... to acquaint their own young children with death ... most shocked of all was the funeral director when mother and daughter went to buy a casket together... private speculation in international exchange rates is useful because it forces governments to face ... reality ... the most recent speculation forced Japan and Germany ... to give the market a greater role in setting exchange rates ... successful official speculation ... would preserve ... existing exchange rates, postpone reality ... and permit economic distortions to grow ... Mary Wells Lawrence ... America's ... highest paid woman executive ... says... "money isn't really what I work for ... money is a flag—you know, success" ... she ... calls herself "one of those lucky people who started work because I had to ... money ... gives you ... a sharp-edged reality that's priceless ... I switch off Friday at about 4 p.m. and don't turn on again until Monday morning ... I have five children and a terrific marriage ... we have practically no social life ... we're like a mini-corporation ... our interests are 100 percent in common. We're both financially oriented and stimulate each other with our thoughts about running a business ... we talk about ... taxes, the stock market, concepts of managing a company, how what's going on in Washington will affect business ... I've always believed that if you're in business, you're in business to make money ... at night ... we don't waste time with social conversation and nobody drinks with each other... we're so tired we don't want to have anything to do with each other"... several persons were concerned that children riding school buses had been able to see nude bathers, and, in one case, a sexual act being performed on top of a car... Bob Lane, school superintendent ... said, "Something has to be done to protect our children from ... the things they see ... get some laws passed that we can enforce and when you, as citizens, serve on a jury, be sure the sentence fits the crime" ... the Texas Lutheran College drama department will stage ...the "Bacchae" with an outdoor setting Tuesday through Saturday ... Gil Garcia, instructor of foreign languages ... will be cast as Dionysos . Walt Maakestad, of Anchorage, Alaska, will play ... Pentheus ... "she ... was a beautiful girl ... the kind of girl a man would want his son to marry ... and Miranda wasn't a bad-looking Mexican. But she was white, and we had a Mormon judge. It was one of those things you can't get away with in Arizona" ... in prison Miranda felt cheated, cheated of his rights, cheated of justice ... Miss Fonda cried "everyday" when she visited North Vietnam. We had bombed their dikes instead of guns placed nearby ... her visits, and those of others like her, caused some of our men to be tortured more ... tears for dikes? It's too bad some restraint can't be placed on Miss Fonda ... cry? My tears are for our men and my rage for what was done to them ... two Cuban exiles ... Reinaldo Pico and Felipe De Diega ... said Saturday they accompanied four of the Watergate conspirators to Washington ... on ... a Central Intelligence Agency mission to disrupt antiwar demonstrations........ both men... said they have worked on and off for the CIA since participating in the Bay of Pigs invasion of Cuba in 1961 ... Pico said he ... was quickly released by police after striking "a long-haired hippie" while Hoover's body lay in state in the Capitol rotunda. "The policeman took me down the stairs of the Capitol and was going to pull me in when a man in a grey suit signalled to let me go" ... "we saw Ellsberg, that traitor, having a victory demonstration during the Hoover funeral and it incensed me," said De Diega. "We started calling them traitors and finally broke up the Ellsberg thing.....the "energy crisis" is really a viciously poisoned onion. Peel off the

108

energy layer and you find the U.S. dollar rapidly losing value year by year. Peel off the money layer and you find the end of the United States as a great power ... present projection shows this country using $24 billion of imported oil in 1980, and more than $30 billion in 1985. These are ... nonsense figures. Bankruptcy ... will come before 1980 unless we change our ways. No one is going to give us such huge amounts of credit every year ... when we cannot possibly pay the money back ... the Persian Gulf states ... will have an oil revenue of at least $16 billion in 1975 and ... in 1980 of about $58 billion ... these are ... nonsense figures. Except for Iran, none of these oil-rich states has the ghost of a serious national defence ... most have tiny population in proportion to their vast riches. History is a harsh process and history will not permit this lunatic situation to endure indefinitely ... such inconceivable wealth cannot pile up indefinitely in such weak hands without stronger hands reaching out from somewhere to take the money away. No nation can continue as a great power when its jugular is overseas ... at the mercy of anyone who comes along with a sharp knife. When

Britain was a great power ... it moved to establish political control of the Persian Gulf. At the same time, Winston Churchill also made the British government the largest single stockholder of the British Petroleum Co., still second in the rank of the huge international oil companies but now without political protection like the rest. All that ended ... in the Suez campaign of 1956. Today, it is the great power role of the United States that is endangered by an exposed jugular overseas. And today, half the nations of the world ... live in independence and go their own ways in relative peace precisely because the United States is still a great power. But maybe not for long ... we buried Grandmother with a deck of cards, pencil and pad, four glasses and a pint ... of bourbon ... why not prepare for the afterlife now? ... when the Day of Reckoning comes she will be ready to start all over again ... wouldn't it be awful if we had to start from scratch as the world once did? ... Sheriff's Deputy William Cramer ... scheduled a police training film, "Play It Cool" ... but when the lights went off ... and the projector began to roll Cramer discovered he had grabbed a canister containing a con-

fiscated 1935 ... pornographic film ... secrecy was enforced on the $100,000 Lockhart State Bank ... robbery ... in spite of rampant rumors ... of what happened inside ... during ... the incident in the heart of the city, only a few feet from the police station ... a reliable source ... said ... the two bandits ... acted as if they were "black militants who hated the whites." The source said the younger bandit threatened to kill the hostages ... or harm them .... the older robber reportedly "kept holding back the younger one, telling him, 'Don't kill 'em. Don't kill 'em'" ... widespread reports circulated ... that one of the robbers raped a woman employee. Bank officials refused to discuss the report ... the source said a rape did occur ... Chief Petrosky ... said, "To the best of my knowledge there was no rape" ... asked ... about the rape ... the FBI replied, "I couldn't comment on that" ... other law enforcement officials would neither confirm nor deny that an employee was raped ... the two bandits held a gun on each side of janitor Eddie Rangel as he arrived at work ... the two men threatened to shoot ... if Rangel closed the door ... most employees already were at work, preparing to open the teller cage ... the vault was open ... the bandits ordered employees to lie on the floor and the two men began filling money bags. Then employees were ordered to enter the vault. Mrs. Jimmie Taylor then arrived for work ...... the bandits reportedly "roughed her up" but did not seriously harm her before locking her in the vault ... the 14 employees in the vault, even though unharmed, might have suffocated ... a fan blowing fresh air into the vault had not been turned on ... four women were hysterical when freed ... The bandits shot up a camera in the ceiling ... they also shot the lock on the door ... they had ... to kick out the glass to leave the building. Five 20-gauge shotgun shells were found inside the door ... the getaway occurred in the brief period ... a ... customer drove to the police station near the bank ... to notify them ... Russo wept on the stand as he recalled the songs of a North Vietnamese prisoner he met. Ellsberg sobbed during a court recess after describing the burning of a South Vietnamese village by its own army ... in 1969 a 230-pound Oakland Raiders linebacker named Chip Oliver adopted a meatless diet to lose some

weight and improve his speed. It worked well enough for him to make first string the last five games of the year. By the opening of the 1970 season however, Oliver was down to 180 pounds and he had lost his interest in football ... much of the non-western world cannot afford meat. About one-third of the world's population does not eat meat ... vegetarian Sylvester Graham, inventor of the Graham cracker .... warned audiences that meat-eating stimulated sexual appetites ... while Dr. John Kellogg, father of the Corn Flake and founder of the dry cereal industry ... lectured, his pet chimp sat nearby contentedly eating a banana. "Eat what the monkeys eat," Kellogg told his audiences. "They are our nearest relatives." Mahatma Gandhi was a strict vegetarian until he came down with a severe case of scurvy ... the shadow of Adolf Hitler flickered across Germany on Good Friday in ... a film depicting the Nazi dictator's last 10 days. The first showing came on what would have been Hitler's 84th birthday. From Munich, where the Nazi movement was born, to Berlin, where Hitler died by his hand, the ... production began without fanfare ... in Munich the Jewish Community Center pro-

tested ... but there was no indication of widespread opposition to the film. Comment ... ranged from "almost macabre" to "fantastic" ... asked what she thought ... an elderly woman who lived through the battle of Berlin replied: "It is a good thing. People should be reminded often that ... Hitler ... almost destroyed us all." "I am too young to have known the Nazi period," said a young man. "That is why I came to see this film. I want to know more" ... the film included the moment ... when Hitler is forced to concede ... "it is all over ... the war is lost ... I am betrayed ... a flaming end for the German people ... they ... failed me ... my Third Reich ... my Third Reich" ... textbook publishers and their salesmen have been known to blanch when Norma Gabler walks into the hearing room. "Don't spoil my sales this year," she quoted one man as saying. "Publish some good textbooks," she answered .... "it seemed to me my children were not learning like they ought to," Mrs. Gabler said. "What really bugged me was that textbooks seem to divide the children from their parents" ... Mrs. Vanderlee ... agreed. "Children seem to be taught to question everything," she said.

"Question your parents. Question authority. I think it makes discipline harder, and I think teachers believe this, too" ... Mrs. Gabler said ... "this chapter, dealing with an Eskimo family, concentrates on cannibalism, infanticide, genocide and senilicide until these acts of violence seem acceptable and understandable to the children . . . there is stabbing, wife stealing, animal beating and mating with all kinds of animals" ... Mrs. Gabler ... quoted the following ... "write a speech of persuasion in which you use selected details to convince your parents to increase your allowance; to give you permission to stay out late at night; to have friends at home when nobody else is at home; to allow you to wear any type of clothing to school." "I know somebody will say that this is teaching children to think," Mrs. Gabler said. "It will—but in the wrong direction. Why are students not asked to do something to please their parents, to help their community or something to better themselves?" ... a new approach to building construction .... a building would be assembled from the foundation up, used, and then when its period of use was over, be disassembled and re-erected somewhere else. Sounds like a handy

option to have in case the neighborhood goes to heck ... former ... POW ... Commander Raymond A. Vohden ... filed ... for divorce, after years of praying for reunion with ... his ... family ... on the table there were letters to his wife from other men, bar bills, cancelled checks and other paraphernalia to back his request ... to end his 13-year-long marriage with Bonnye Jean Vohden ... he said ... "over there family love was something ... you could grasp at ... my ankle was crippled and I couldn't kneel but each night I lay on my straw mat under my mosquito net and told God that if my wife was waiting for me ... I would worship him thankfully every Sunday that I was alive ... POWs' wives ... seem to have similar behavioral patterns. They admit to relationships with other men that we regard as misconduct but which they see as the inevitable consequence ... four of my close friends I shared cells with are facing major ... marital ... difficulties." Vohden phoned his wife and demanded to know the truth. "She told me there was another man, but to come home and talk about it ... Bonnye Jean was ... waiting ... in a limousine ... I gave her a hug and a kiss, but ... she ... was

cool ... not like she was there waiting for me ... I was going through her things in her bedroom, looking for old mementoes. And I came across some pictures of her with other men, some letters and cancelled checks and the bitterness rose in me ... I want my house, I could never stand another man living in my house" ... the day her husband was released ... Bonnye Jean talked to him ... and later told reporters, "He sounded as mean as ever" ... Dear Father Lester: How do you reconcile freedom of speech and ... those 'sex-talk' radio shows where the interviewer chats with unidentified women about the most intimate details of their sex lives? ...... freedom of speech is not unlimited ... all knowledge, in the abstract, is good. But concrete circumstances can change some knowledge from good to bad ... even for the reasonably mature person to be swamped with phantasms and talk about sex can be a shove in the wrong direction. Hence, if "sex-talk" radio shows would normally be detrimental to the immature or would encourage adults to evil ... the shows ordinarily would have no right to be aired ... the judge told the court stenographer, "Let the record show that the defendant has asked the court to appoint counsel ... and the court declined the request" ... I'm 48 years old and experiencing menopause ... when I have hot flashes or feel uncomfortable, I try to hide it ... in our family ... hiding things is the best policy ... after our oldest boy died ... I would go down to the backyard ... and cry. I also read a lot ... my husband stayed away from home except to sleep and sometimes not even for that (he told his friends I was difficult ... because I was having 'change of life' ...). I've waited over 25 years ... and ... now he's showing kindness ... I'm afraid to rock the boat by telling him I really am in menopause ... six of our children still live at home ... once in a while, I get this sadness in me about my son, but still I feel I have to conceal it from my husband. I cover ... up by joking and making him laugh. Is there any help for me? ... losing a son causes ... deep and lasting grief ... stop questioning this loss ... you're doing yourself and your family a disservice by not disclosing ... that you are going through menopause. If you were more open ... you ... would ... relax ... and ... get rid ... of those ... devastating ... inner tensions ... see your doctor ... if you follow

... these approaches ... you and your family ... will ... feel better ... University of Texas psychologist Dr. Horn ... said ... his study indicates that persons gravitate to various academic disciplines because of certain personality traits ... he contends that personality factors over a period of years may unduly influence the composition and direction of a given profession ... certain kinds of students may be attracted to engineering because it is "a data-oriented field not given to arm-chair theorizing," while ... psychology is characterized by " a lot of ambiguity and a plethora of contradictory ideas and theories." Dr. Horn found a high correlation between the anxiety-proneness of psychology students and ... belief that external events shape peoples' lives. "To the degree that such factors might interfere with a psychologist's objectivity," Dr. Horn said, "it could be bad for scientific discipline" ... ... Mrs. Bonnell Sybert, teller at the First National Bank of Jarrell, was counting the bank's money ..... when she heard a man's voice say ... "lady, this is a stick up" ... the Lockhart bank robbery had been discussed all morning by Mrs. Sybert with ... her ... customers. "We were wondering when it

would happen here ... and ... if we could get out of the vault if it was locked behind us" ... Emil Danek, owner of Danek Hardware just across the street from the Bank ... provided ... police ... with a car description and license plate number ... Danek ... saw the car stop at the bank about 11:30 a.m. and noticed the out-of-state plates ..... his interest was aroused when the man "switched something under his shirt" after getting out of the auto. Danek ... speculated later that the man was putting a pistol under his shirt ... he ... walked across the street and wrote down the license plate number on a match box. "I don't know what I was doing it for," Danek said later. He said he often noted the license numbers of unfamiliar automobiles "in case something happens." Wednesday was the first time anything happened to make the practice pay off ... an FBI agent at the scene ... said ... "if we break it (the case), it'll be because ... Danek ... was on the ball" ... the Jarrell State Bank ... founded in 1911 ... is in the center of Jarrell, a town of 400. Weeds are sprouting in front of the pink brick building whose glossy black tile facade is slowly chipping away ... there are still people who object to the flagrant display of nude

112

bodies in public. Behind closed doors, fine, perhaps. In public in front of us and our families without our consent, no ... I do not see the necessity for a lot of gobbledygook for a sex-saturated society to hide behind. They certainly don't hide when they want some nude swimming so why give them something they can hide behind in the law ... I am sick and tired of everyone talking in hushed tones about what's going on, so hold on ... a busload of children ... saw two nudes in full view in sex on top of a car parked along the road on private property. A neighbor who walked into her backyard to empty trash saw two nude couples engaged in the sex act ... a man taking a casual morning stroll saw a nude black male and two white nude females engaged in sex ... the grandmother of a nine-year-old girl witnessed two nude men standing in full view while motioning to the girl and her seven-year-old girl friend from a secluded area nearby. A man driving down the road saw a nude girl, lying along the county road easement, apparently out of her mind from drugs. A family ... can't look out of their living room windows for seeing nudes walk by ... convince me this sort of conduct in pub-

lic is sanctioned by the majority of our citizens, and I'll say God help us all. The ecologists and the naturalists can yell all they want about wanting the area left untouched and undeveloped. That's a lot of humbug. What they really want is to be left alone so they can finish destroying this country and take over this area —untouched by the law. Somebody had better do something before it's too late ... the well-heeled woman with a yen for freedom has discovered Sun Valley ... a resort where it's almost as easy to break up a marriage in the courts as it is to break a leg on the slopes ... Sun Valley—with a year-round population of 180—is far from a mecca for would-be divorcees ... "we don't want this to become a divorce mill like Reno," said Attorney Everett "Phez" Taylor ... "we want only the carriage trade, not the bus trade ... it's fairly amicable" ... Idaho lawyers get a minimum $500 or $1000 fee. Costs and isolation keep the clientele limited ... comfortable housing to wait out the six ... week residency can cost as much as $4000. A private ski instructor at $50 a day, massage, dining out, shopping in ... boutiques and other pleasures ... double the divorce bill. And those

who've stayed in Sun Valley say it's really fun if you know the right people ... Mrs. J. had been married almost 30 years when her husband asked for a divorce. Anxious to marry again he offered to send her to Sun Valley ... said Mrs. J. who took a three bedroom condominium, costing $60 a day ... "I have lots of friends here so I'm ... never lonely. I go cross-country skiing, take a swim, have a massage, go shopping. Time passes quickly and there's no excuse ever to be bored ... Reno sounded too dreary. This is the only place I considered coming to ... besides he's paying for it all" ... full-time resident .... Gee Nowakoski ... recalled ... "There seems to be a stream of women coming here ... for the Marlboro man to ride off into the sunset with ... them ... but ... you can be as social as you want here. It's easy for a single woman to get around." Happy Murphy, now Mrs. Nelson Rockefeller, Pat Kennedy Lawford, and Ann McDonnell Ford lived here during their separation. So did Charlotte Ford Niarchos (who will soon be marrying Tony Forstmann, whose ex-wife continued to live in Sun Valley after their divorce) ... last year's Sun Valley celebrity ... was ... New

York socialite Amanda Burdon ... visitors ... have included the shah of Iran ... Barbara Streisand, Mrs. Aristotle Onassis, and Ethel Kennedy. It's fine company to enjoy and ... women ... make sure their stay is relatively care-free by deciding property settlement and child custody with their lawyers at home ... before coming ... one bell-hop ... explained, "Most of these women are very nice and we get to know them well ... of course we know what ... they're ... there for ... I remember a Mrs. Moore who stayed in a room costing $75 a day. She was great fun and gave all kinds of parties for the employees. As a rule, though, most ... women ... are too socially conscious to mix with the employees. After drinking and dining with someone all night, you feel kind of strange when she asks you to pick up her laundry the next morning." Many women use the six weeks to learn or perfect their skiing. The resort has top-rate Austrian instructors whose good looks almost match their ... technique ... a woman ... may ... spot a particularly handsome ski instructor and request him for six weeks of private instruction. Friendships develop well beyond the slopes ... some instruc-

tors say they are left ... expensive gifts and tips as high as $1000. "It's not surprising that a woman might fall in love with a ski instructor," said Australian Russell Howden, 34 ... he stood in the crowded Ram Bar, having changed from his orange ski parka and boots into a red turtle neck sweater and white track shoes. "You're spending ... time with ... a woman ... who looks up to you and admires you for your skill. And it's all happening in an exotic atmosphere" ... "we get such nice women out here," says Dorise ... Phez ... Taylor's ... wife ... "they all come out here with their typewriters and their French lessons, all set to work ... and ... they ... just end up enjoying beautiful Sun Valley." Glenn Cooper moved out ... on her husband ...... several years ago with her 5 children. "There just couldn't be a more beautiful place to live as a single woman with children. You can ... get close to them and create a solid family unit. And I've had such good things happen to me," says Mrs. Cooper, who is now busy organizing the Creative Arts Center. "I left my marriage uncertain and insecure, but here I've really had a chance to grow" ... visitors to the Troy area are always

asking: "Where's the Trojan Horse?" So Turkey is building a new one, 35 feet high, near the spot where the original Trojan Horse is believed to have entered the city 3,200 years ago ... "the disastrous engine was jockeyed through our walls, an army in its womb," the Roman poet Vergil quoted an ancient Trojan as saying. At night the Greeks climbed out and wiped out Troy ... tourists will be able to enter the pinewood horse, climbing a 14-foot ladder ... where they can ... get an idea of what it was like to be an ancient Greek in the belly of a wooden horse .... Ghana's government which repudiated $94 million of its debts to western creditors 14 months ago and demanded that its entire $300 million medium-term debt be rescheduled, has so far shown no willingness to back down on its decision despite concerted international effort ... Ghana reiterated its stand repudiating $94 million it owes four British firms. Ghana's action has raised great concern in Washington, London and other European capitals because officials fear a dangerous precedent will be set if Ghana gets away with repudiating such a large debt ... Ghana feels ... it is high time that the rules of the

114

international lending game are radically changed so that poor nations are not drained of their resources in the process of repaying their debts ... Dear Father Lester ... do people "win the right to be their own masters?" Didn't you say people are born with the right? ... people have the right through nature to be their own masters. The right, of course, is limited by divine, natural and civil effort. Sometimes people are unaccustomed to uniting for community effort. These naturally need a strong leader who can tell them what they should do for the good of the community. The dictator, though, must seek to put the rule of the country into the hands of the people as soon as practicality will allow ... "that Asiatic city of innumerable churches, Holy Moscow!" According to Tolstoy's "War and Peace," Napoleon uttered these words as he stood before Moscow and directed his army's invasion in September 1812. A visitor to Moscow today doesn't see nearly as many gilded, onion-shaped cupolas as Napoleon saw ... many churches ... were destroyed in orgies of atheism under Stalin and Nikita Khrushchev. Some suffered more ignominious fates: They were turned into

museums, aquariums, movie theaters, clubs, furniture factories, offices or apartments. And still others dotting the landscape are only abandoned .... one chilly afternoon, two elderly women in woolen shawls paused silently in the Kremlin's opulent Archangel Cathedral and crossed themselves. "This is a museum," a young woman guide was telling a group of foreign visitors ... "only a few old people from another generation come here for religious purposes" ..... Operation Homecoming—the repatriation of 596 Americans from Indochinese prison camps—has been an emotional experience... .... first came joy. Pictures of wives breaking through barriers to dive into their husbands' arms ..... then came anger. With ..... the POW's free to tell their gruesome story of torture, joy turned to outrage—and pride ...that ... these men had not only survived the ... savagery of their captors but somehow retained ... their discipline and their faith ... it is too soon to judge what all this has done to the national psyche. A bath of this kind must do something. Possibly something invigorating ... these men may ... make prideful patriotism respectable again ... the wife ...... of a Department of Public

Safety narcotics officer ... told police she was raped ... repeatedly ...... early Thursday morning by a man who ... wanted to "get even" with her husband. Wearing a ski mask and gloves the man entered her home just before 4 a.m. ... apparently through an unlocked door. The assault took place ...... while her three small children slept in a nearby room. Her assailant was armed ... with a small steak knife ... he ... told her he knew her husband was out of town ... on a case ... Senator Barry Goldwater ... in addition to the phone calls and letters you have been getting from Republican leaders on Watergate ... what is their basic anxiety? A. Well, it's what a job it makes for them ... it's giving us troubles. I hope we can get out of it ... I am 18, have long blonde hair, am 5 feet, 3 inches, with measurements of 37-26-38. I graduated from high school with honors. I own over $700 in jewelry ... a stereo, a color TV, and a closet full of beautiful clothes ... I've gone steady six times, have received five class rings, a bracelet, a necklace, a sweetheart ring, five and a half dozen roses, two boxes of candy and many, many love letters ... I've gone through 40 boys in 2-and-1/2 years! I found only one that I wanted to keep. And he didn't want ME! ... I'm never satisfied ... as soon as I get something ... I don't want it. I'm proud of the fact that I've never gone all the way. All my friends have dates, but I don't have anyone and I'm so jealous I could die. Please help me ... testimony in the trial ... indicated Curtis and the narcotics officer who arrested him, Police Sgt. George B. Shephard, had struggled on the floor behind a counter in Curtis' record store. It was ... then ... a nine gram packet containing heroin was found in Curtis' mouth ... defense attorney ... Spivey suddenly dropped to the floor in front of the jury box. He spoke for a moment from the floor, invisible to the jury, drawing the analogy that Shephard and Curtis had been just as invisible when the heroin was found ... officers inside the shop ... had talked with Curtis off and on some 25 minutes before the heroin was found ... Spivey turned his back a moment, then faced the jury again. This time he had something in his mouth and mumbled an argument that if Curtis had had a package of heroin in his mouth, he would not have been able to talk intelligibly with the officers. Spivey removed the package ... and showed the jury

that it was a 50 cent piece wrapped in plastic ... Spivey ... said most people see a narcotics officer as a man "swinging through the trees of crime with an American flag in his right hand" .... he referred to the incident as "a true wrong in our community" ... Curtis, 29, was found guilty about 10 p.m. Wednesday by a seven-man, five-woman jury. As the jury was leaving the courthouse, one juror was assaulted by a spectator ... the juror was slammed against the wall and hit on the head ... on the second floor landing of the courthouse stairs as he walked down from the fourth floor courtroom ... one courthouse source ... said it took deputies "30 to 40 minutes" to clear the courtroom after the guilty verdict was returned ... "it looked like there might be bad trouble for a while" ... Travis County Judge H. Watson had to break a 2-2 tie vote Monday morning to bring about approval of a resolution urging a law against public nudity ... Watson said, "The resolution probably is moot and immaterial, but I see no harm in it, so I'll vote for it" ... two of the four commisioners, Richard Moya and Johnny Voudouris, refused to sign the resolution. Of the section declaring

that nudity in and around such places as "Hippie Hollow" on Lake Travis was affecting the morals of children, Voudouris later said, "I suppose my morals were ruined because when I was in the Cub Scouts we used to skinny-dip" ... American prisoners of war began rehearsing patriotic speeches two years ago, in a prison camp exercise some of them called "reverse brainwashing" ... "it made us ardent anti-communists for the most part and ultra-patriotic," said Webb, who had spent five years as a prisoner ... "it's awful hard to spend six, seven, eight years of that and come out ...... for naught," Hiteshaw added. "That would be pretty difficult and we'd be a bitter bunch" .... in the main prison camp ..... dubbed the "Hanoi Hilton" by its inmates, downed American airmen formed several toastmaster clubs and practiced public speaking ... the toastmaster clubs even staged news conferences, with some prisoners playing the parts of reporters and asking barbed questions, while others rehearsed the roles they are actually playing now ... Webb said ... "the only thing you had to fall back on was basic faith, faith in God, faith in your country, in your family, in your

116

way of life ... there were many of us, for example, who were conservative Republicans ... and ... we'd defend Lyndon Johnson and the Democratic administration to the hilt rather than accede to their crackpot propaganda" ... "we were always behind the administration," Hiteshaw said, "regardless of who it was" ... the pro-administration line taken by most former POW's has led to charges that they were delivering speeches prepared for them. But to a man they deny this ... "it was very definitely reverse brainwashing," Webb concluded ... the most recent coup in Ghana was conducted by Col. Ignatius Kutu Acheampong .... Acheampong pronounced the ... $94 million ... obligation to England ... null and void on the grounds that it had been incurred through corruption. Whee! ... Acheampong went further and nationalized over half of his country's foreign-owned gold, diamond and timber operations. But suddenly things began to happen. Credit dried up—completely. Forced to pay cash for its imports, Ghana's prices skyrocketed. In no time at all, Acheampong was crawling back to the creditors ... in Europe they've been around a long time, and when they lend out

money, they get it back or else ... and ... there are very few gasps of outrage from other than the kind of people who howl out their discontents in Hyde Park ... there is the small girl, about four, who came walking home one day with both hands cut off and a sign around her neck warning her father, a hamlet chief, and his associates they could expect more of this if they persisted in opposing the Viet Cong ... there is the priest, from a Catholic church, as I recall, whose body was found slit in half up and down, half nailed to the wall of the church, half to a fence some distance away ... there was the practice, common some years ago, of the VC starting a ruckus outside a village, drawing the police out, then moving into the rear and systematically killing or torturing their wives and children ... I guess Jane Fonda never saw these bodies ... current U.S. policy in the Mideast is designed to convince the Palestinian people that Yassir Arafat and other strident guerrilla leaders are radicalizing the Palestinian organizations ... the policy could serve to separate the masses from the extremist leaders who ... represent ... advocacy of terror tactics against the United States ... Arafat's threats of "big

vengeance" for U.S. collaboration ... are considered a classic case of a militant hogging the world spotlight and inhibiting others from speaking ... the United States is working around leaders like Arafat to reach the Palestinians ... most of whom are believed to favor an accomodation with Israel providing the Palestinians are granted their own province ... the Palestinian ... masses are considered the "silent majority" ... theirs is the unheard voice of moderation ... realistic Palestinians are in the majority ... extremist leaders ... understand this fully. The terror tactics typified by explosions Saturday at an American-owned oil storage terminal ... are seen as an attempt to sabotage any start towards a peaceful settlement ... "how does it feel to just bomb women and children?" someone asked former prisoner of war Richard Stratton ... the Navy commander answered ... "the Vietnamese ... chose ... to hide behind the skirts of women and children ... they are counting on your Christian concepts to allow them to operate freely ...their government selected it. Their government must be held responsible" ... shot down ... during a January 1967 combat

117

mission, Stratton was pictured two months later bowing to unseen captors. A Life magazine photographer ... heard Stratton admit that anti-personnel bombing was used to intimidate the populated areas of Hanoi ... Fahr Aints (eng. Fire Ants): Fearsomely powerful rural Texas vermin capable of raising 100 times their own weight in appropriations ... Russo ... said he ... was indicted because he refused to testify in secret to a federal grand jury investigating the case. About that refusal which led to his being jailed for 47 days in 1971, Russo has said: "My testifying in secret would have been collaborating with a star chamber proceeding ... I had a story to tell and I wanted my day in court, but I wanted it to be public" ... "the cops here are really pretty nice. I heard they were down on kids but I think they're cooler than the cops back home," one young man said ... newly-elected Fort Lauderdale Mayor Shuman Young ... 56 ... is concerned ... that foul-mouthed and ill-kempt "bums" ... give the city a bad image ... the beach isn't just 'Where The Boys Are' ... young women were outnumbered 20 to 1 ... said the Mayor: "the beach is for everyone. It's for

the bums, too ... but we can't let them take over ... we're a city of 180,000 and we've got something for old people, working people, everyone—not just kids" ... [my landlord writes the editor:] I am sick and tired of the pleas I hear for trees in the development ... of our city. Those persons who have dedicated themselves, professionally, to the development of our land for homes and shops, and schools, are being strangled by a minority of true characters ...... O.K. ... I'm a realtor. I love trees ... you just try riding about this beautiful city ..... and look at the trees—millions of 'em—better still, fly ... and you view a veritable sea of foliage! Now, before we, as a city, stamped out the subdivisions ...... there was a great mass of tree coverage—oaks, pecan, cedar and mesquite. We needed ... land and blip, the trees were cleared! Yeh! Even like they do today out in the country! ... most folks live in houses these days—in subdivisions. I like to recall the old McElroy Ranch .... 400 acres in the northwest part of the city ... bordered, approximately, by ... Burnet Road (east), Greenlawn Parkway (south), Balcones Drive (west) and Anderson Lane (north). [and almost smack dab in the middle of all this:

my rent house! —C.D.] ... I sold ... the ranch ... for development about 14 years ago. I can still see that gentle, sloping, barren pasture with white-faced Herefords ... today ... there are trees covering the same land plus hundreds of fine homes of fine folks, along with churches, schools and parks. Yep, people plant trees ... they ... feed them, and spray them, admire them and enjoy them ... I see more trees via development ... for my city. So why are we allowing the continued harassment and petty debate ... not one concerned citizen (builder, subdivider, or realtor) could be ... accused of maliciously destroying a great oak or pecan or cypress ... some trees ... die during ... drought or ... disease— some are uprooted by the wind, but material things are expendable and can be replaced. My response to the group creating all the problems is that you are not concerned about people other than your own recognition and your continued efforts negate the truly honest endeavors of those providing for the citizenry ... the Lebanese Revolutionary Guard said the attack ... on an American-owned oil refinery in Southern Lebanon ... was "intended to blow up the unholy alliance between the United States, Saudi Arabia and Lebanon that is directed against the lives and independence of our people. Oil feeds imperialism and goes into planes and other destructive weapons ... which the United States is supplying our oppressors generously ....Senator Goldwater added ... "now John Dean happens to be an old roommate of my son's. And I've talked to him. I've never pumped him. But I asked him, 'Is there any truth in this?' And he said, 'Not at all.' And I believe this kid" ... do you know what April showers bring, Priscilla? Yeh ... a good bawling-out if I get my feet wet ... the cancer death rate rose in 1972 at the fastest pace in 22 years, the National Center for Health Statistics has reported. Experts offered various explanations but agreed that increased exposure to cancer-causing chemicals in man's environment—his air, water, soil and food—probably was involved ... the rate of increase is 3.35 per cent or about triple the annual average since 1950 ... death of two brethren from drinking strychnine has cast a pall over a little Holiness Church flock ... but ... they will continue to test their faith with snakes, poison and even fire ...... both were buried with a Bible in

their caskets open at the passage in the Gospel of St. Mark which reads: "They shall take up serpents and if they drink any deadly thing, it shall not hurt them" ... anyone for Atlantis? A big expedition to search for that lost continent is forming ... to comb the bottom of the Atlantic, off Cadiz, Spain ... what makes this ... expedition ... unique is that it is using a combination of science and the psychic .... but the psychics are no more important than the scientists. All known information about the area has been computerized, and, as they go along, everything else they find and learn will be fed into the computer, too ..... Ms. Asher ...... head of the search team ... who says ... "Atlantis isn't a mystery ... any longer" ... thinks she has it pinpointed ... in her mind ... other scientists are looking ... Russian scientists acknowledge the existence of Atlantis and ... Ms. Asher ... hopes to beat them to proving it ... in 1967 ... Anghelos Galanopoulos discovered a prehistoric Cretan-type city on the Greek island of Thera and promptly declared he had found Atlantis. Ms. Asher feels that the claim is erroneous and cites carbon dating ... which proves ..... Thera ..... flourished about 1500 B.C.

Atlantis was ... considerably older than that. She believes that the Thera site is a "Greek effort to attract tourists" and hints that there is a world-famous Greek millionaire behind the effort there. She says that Galanopoulos ... has made overtures to join her expedition, but she isn't sure whether or not she'll ask him ... Ms. Asher has long been fascinated with "the common origin of man" but never really thought much about Atlantis until the big ... Los Angeles ... earthquake of February, 1971 ... two things fell from her shelves that shaky morning ... a book on Atlantis ... and ... a statue of a Cretan goddess. From that morning on, she's been working steadily to put this ... expedition ... together ... there is ... much evidence that Atlantis really did exist— such things as similarity of languages without a seeming common origin, megaliths of the same general character in varying locations, and "concentric spirals." This curious design has been found on islands on both sides of the Atlantic, and Plato speaks of Atlantis as a "spiral city ... North by Northwest beyond the Pillars of Hercules," the ancients' name for the Straits of Gibraltar ... a prisoner from El Reno Federal Reformatory led authorities to the ... shallow ... grave of Celeste Lee St. Dizier, 18 ... police said ... that another man had given Celeste a heavy dose of narcotics to knock her out during a seduction attempt. The drugs apparently killed her. Celeste had disappeared June 23, 1972 ... "she told me that night she was going to a party and then to Fort Worth the next day to see the Rolling Stones concert" ... the mother ... Mrs. St. Dizier said ... "the worst part was wondering if she was sick, or hurt, or being held prisoner somewhere" ... Mrs. St. Dizier said she did not know whether police would find the man who gave her daughter the narcotics, but added: "I'll never stop looking" ... Sioux helicopters of the British army's Blue Eagles display team carry out a "bomb burst" maneuver over . . .

Stonehenge ... the controversial ... landmark in Salisbury, England ... the ... FBI ... said there apparently is no connection between the Jarrell robbery Wednesday and another bank holdup in Lockhart the day before ... nude sunbathing ... is now spreading ... Sunday (April 1) totally nude sunbathers invaded private property to put themselves on public display at Travis Vista, almost at the back door of the Marshall Ford Baptist Church. Other nude sunbathers were displaying themselves at Hughes County Park near Saint Luke's Episcopal Church ... give them an inch and they'll take a mile. Give them Hippie Hollow, and they'll take all of Lake Travis. Give them Lake Travis—and what will be next? ... in all this world, Charlie Brown, there is nothing more frightening than the

group of parents ... in bridge ...... the odds against getting a perfect deal (a 13-card suit for each of the four players) are 2,235,197,406,895, 366,368,301,599,999 to 1. The perfect deal (13 spades for you, 13 hearts at your left, 13 diamonds for your partner and 13 clubs at your right—naming the suit for each hand) occurs 24 times less frequently. That comes to 53 followed by 27 figures. A perfect hand (a 13-card suit) occurs once every 158,753,389,900 times. By the most optimistic reckoning, we should have a perfect hand in the United States or Canada about once every ten years—assuming that most of us played bridge like mad instead of doing the things we usually do. Then why do we get these reports of perfect hands every year—usually with the coming of Spring?

10. Rising

"the sign of the light"

whether
lamp
fire
sun

do not let go

star
diamond
crystal
dark circle
point
finger

again
moon full face
noon sun
eyes
mist
wind
glow worm
smoke
jewels

shining hands touch the head

light of the head

clear without qualities colorless void

body's heat rises

listen

"sees"

a light in the heart

dawn

the clear light

the young man on the rope

is cut to pieces

thrown into waves of liquid quartz

he falls to earth

fragments broken from his throne

the flying tree

red man white man straining smeared with chalk

eat and you will be like me

want to?

"except for the light that shines from the eyes"

lightning

through darkness into secrets

stolen souls in far lands

bones glowing through flesh

flesh a vapor of fire

mind outside

enclosing the body in a kernel of flame

"now"

inside crystal

the soul wandering in scrub

to see them

123

ascend a ladder of glass

angels and devils settling the balance

copper flash

don't ask questions

the morning star

when there is no noon

the tree flies

the bee gathers honey with our tongue

they live undefinedly

death feels the flash

thousand suns at once

"I am become death"

diadems maces discus immeasurable

124

middle end where?

mouth of fire terrible with long teeth

I do not know the four quarters

I do not find peace

eternal boy

with a sword of light he cuts open the dark cloud of the woman

they cross ocean between two walls of water

mist   horse stop

suspended in water

they are touched and walk out

strike   the mist

dissolves

or else an egg a vapor a web of cloth a clay ball

by penetration the final deliverance

to the north of the "Milky Ocean"

White Island

Leukē Avalon

the brightness of one man

the last explosion of life

light rising

the glory that blinds

yellow and white

winking inside the sea of the woman

wearing each other's clothes

bodies that shine like silver

living in palaces of gold

"I have become flame"

fire wings

"I have risen into air"

                           tuft of hair catlick on my head
what do I know that makes it shine?

            by knowing light shines
        through the mouths of the body

five lights at birth   a flame from the corpse

          like a brand struck in the game

       photon tachyon

               in a cave in the mountain
                         fiery joy
             singing
               . mouth open
           stone rolled back

     "the sun escapes"

grown one like two trees

a troop of gods

witness
play
sparkle
laugh

dancing fire   sun game

cave a column of light above fingers playing with spirits

          "hep"   four

                              the yellow flower

   blue light an egg

 satisfied by sight

          darkening by touch

   white light an egg stepping out hand in hand the male female

             a plume of five-starred light

    work and death and play

mimicking is not repeating

illusion no shadow

deadening brings deliverance

earth sinks into water

shakes her back

returns

upheld on the low cups of sun

"by which she sees herself"

otherwise like talking to a mirror

swimming against the river

pushing against the sky

axle
beanstalk
navel

either in a cave or coming down off a mountain top

star

that darkens the sun

will lead

over field past fountains across plains to the child

face shining

the ocean

the dragon

"more in those few seconds than any previous study"

the body is unpropped

unstrung marionette

limbs flop

crooked dice

"stands stood will stand"

a veil like the moon's

then the sun's

night

blind

lightning

on the fourth day "deep blues"

dull white from the spirits beats against your eyes

guns fire

you can't hear them

avoid

for six more days

choosing a light

entering a womb

                        white   blue

then   yellow   red

                            finally all the light together

                                        the fingers

servant breath "out of the body"

                    five folded spray into the funnels

                            without loss of time

            pearl on the tip of his rod

                                        "drop"